Do the Next Thing

A Manual on Dealing with the Fear of Cancer

Glen R. Jackson

Copyright © 2015 Glen Robert Jackson and Nicki Jackson.

All rights reserved. No part of this book may be used or reproduced by any means, graphic, electronic, or mechanical, including photocopying, recording, taping or by any information storage retrieval system without the written permission of the publisher except in the case of brief quotations embodied in critical articles and reviews.

WestBow Press books may be ordered through booksellers or by contacting:

WestBow Press
A Division of Thomas Nelson & Zondervan
1663 Liberty Drive
Bloomington, IN 47403
www.westbowpress.com
1 (866) 928-1240

Because of the dynamic nature of the Internet, any web addresses or links contained in this book may have changed since publication and may no longer be valid. The views expressed in this work are solely those of the author and do not necessarily reflect the views of the publisher, and the publisher hereby disclaims any responsibility for them.

Any people depicted in stock imagery provided by Thinkstock are models, and such images are being used for illustrative purposes only.
Certain stock imagery © Thinkstock.

ISBN: 978-1-4908-7560-6 (sc)
ISBN: 978-1-4908-7562-0 (hc)
ISBN: 978-1-4908-7561-3 (e)

Library of Congress Control Number: 2015905267

Print information available on the last page.

WestBow Press rev. date: 08/06/2015

Contents

Foreword ix
Chapter 1 1
Chapter 2 2
Chapter 3 4
Chapter 4 8
Chapter 5 10
Chapter 6 13
Chapter 7 15
Chapter 8 18
Chapter 9 20
Chapter 10 23
Chapter 11 26
Chapter 12 29
Chapter 12b 32
Chapter 13 33
Chapter 14 35
Chapter 15 38
Chapter 16 41
Chapter 17 42
Chapter 18 44
Chapter 19 45
Chapter 20 46
Chapter 21 48
Chapter 22 50

Chapter 23 51
Chapter 24 53
Chapter 25 55
Chapter 26 56
Chapter 27 57
Chapter 28 59
Chapter 29 61
Chapter 30 63
Chapter 31 65
Chapter 32 67
Chapter 33 69
Chapter 34 71
Chapter 35 73
Chapter 36 75
Chapter 37 76
Chapter 38 78
Chapter 39 80
Chapter 40 81
Chapter 41 83
Chapter 42 85
Chapter 43 87
Chapter 44 89
Chapter 45 90
Chapter 46 92
Chapter 47 93
Chapter 48 95
Chapter 49 97
Chapter 50 98
Chapter 51 100
Chapter 52 102
Chapter 53 103
Chapter 54 104
Chapter 55 106
Chapter 56 107

Chapter 57 108
Chapter 58 109
Chapter 59 110
Chapter 60 111
Chapter 61 113
Chapter 62 116
Chapter 63 118
Chapter 64 120
Chapter 65 122
Chapter 66 123
Chapter 67 124
Chapter 68 125
Chapter 69 127
Chapter 70 129
Chapter 71 130
Chapter 72 132
Chapter 73 135
Chapter 74 136
Chapter 75 137
Chapter 76 139
Chapter 77 140
Chapter 78 141
Chapter 79 142
Chapter 80 143
Chapter 81 145
Chapter 82 146
Chapter 83 147
Chapter 84 148
Epilogue 151
Notes 157
Acknowledgements 159

Foreword

As a physician and cancer specialist, I am constantly looking for new resources for myself and for my patients. I personally have gained a great deal of insight from reading *Do the Next Thing*. This is a practical manual for both the cancer patient and the caregiver. By emphasizing the spiritual, Pastor Jackson turns the trial of battling cancer into a means for spiritual elevation. This book addresses and answers questions that every patient asks but often not to medical professionals. Too frequently, the health care provider glosses over the emotional component of a patient's fight against cancer. *Do the Next Thing* provides an intimate look at this dynamic from the perspective of a loving husband and a man of faith. I truly feel that individuals with cancer, their caregivers, and medical professionals will all benefit greatly from the anecdotes and advice so wittily and accurately shared in this work.

Victor Schweitzer, MD
Radiation Oncologist

Every year, millions of people in our nation die because of cancer. The pain and grief caused by this disease are incalculable. The good news is that far more people diagnosed with cancer now are surviving.

This book is dedicated to those who have committed their lives to bring healing to people suffering through this terrible disease.

To the doctors, nurses, and technicians who spend years studying and learning about ways to make cancer as rare as polio.

To those who encourage individuals and families going through this disease with kind words, simple cards, e-mail notes, meals, financial support, and visits.

To the prayer warriors who battle all diseases on another sphere, most of whom will not be known this side of eternity but who fight the battle in the trenches every day.

To our Savior, who was *"a man of sorrows and acquainted with grief"* (Isaiah 53:3 NASB).

To the Praying Pastors of Simi Valley, who have walked this path with us.

To my family, who have stuck with us through this entire ordeal.

And especially to Nicki, who makes my heart beat faster every time I walk into her presence and who gives my life such meaning. It has been an honor to serve her through this valley.

Chapter 1

On Valentine's Day, I gave my wife a mammogram as a gift; it saved her life.

Chapter 2

My wife, Nicki, is my best friend. We met while serving on the staff of a large church in Los Gatos, California. She was the senior pastor's administrative assistant, and I worked in the youth department. It was not love at first sight. Over the course of five years, she had several boyfriends. I was not one of them; however, we did go out on many "friend dates." There would be a church outing, and she wouldn't have a date, so we would go together. A movie would come out, and we would go together to see it. We became friends but were not serious about each other.

On February 12, I told her I thought I loved her and asked if I could kiss her. She was surprised that I kissed well. Two days later, on Valentine's Day, having Chateaubriand for two in an exclusive restaurant overlooking a beautiful lake, she broke up with me. Then we got back together. Then we broke up. It was a very confusing time.

About this time, I was contacted by an Indianapolis church about joining their staff as a youth minister. I spent a weekend with their leadership to ask questions and to discern the available opportunities. When asked if I had a girlfriend, I replied that I did not. After I returned to San Jose, Nicki picked me up at the airport, and we went out for a bowl of soup and discussion. I talked about the weekend and the possibilities that were before me. I was excited about my future. She then asked me a question that changed our lives.

"What about me?"

Up to that moment, that question did not enter the equation of what was planned for my future. Before I left for Indianapolis, she had told me that we were not dating, so any decision made would not include her. At least, I thought it did not include her. While I was gone for the weekend, she began to think about the relationship that we had developed. I was safe and dependable, just not exciting. However, she began to put everything into perspective and realized that safe and dependable was a good thing. Her heart began to melt, and we were engaged two days later. My call back to Indiana informing them that their new youth minister who did not have a girlfriend was now engaged caught them by surprise. I received a $500 raise.

In a period of five weeks, I would graduate from college, be ordained, get married, go on a honeymoon, and move from California to Indiana. Such has been our life. It has been a busy life filled with stress, complications, joy, two daughters, friends, and lots of love. It is the life we chose for ourselves. More precisely, it is the life God planned for us.

Our plan did not include cancer.

Chapter 3

Cancer affects everyone differently. Some go into denial. Some go into the blame game. Some look for unproven cures and health gurus. We chose to attack the cancer with abandon. As Christians, we believe God allowed this to occur. Our faith was never in doubt, and we never blamed God for anything. We went to Him and sought His direction and received peace and strength. The Bible says, *"And we know that for those who love God all things work together for good, for those who are called according to His purpose"* (Romans 8:28 ESV). We have found this to be true. While we never sought this disease, God used it in many ways to demonstrate His love in our lives.

Our battle with cancer began in April. After receiving her gift certificate, Nicki called and made an appointment for a mammogram. When she made her appointment, the center asked if this was an urgent matter or a regular appointment. Nicki had a mammogram two years prior, so there did not seem to be a rush. The next opening was in April, so the appointment was set. A week after her test, we received a letter stating:

"Based on the images obtained, there is an area on your right breast ultrasound for which the radiologist recommended further evaluation. This is in order to obtain a more definite diagnosis than that provided by imaging alone. Further tests, including stereotactic/ultrasound guided biopsy, are being recommended by the radiologists."

For a woman, that can be a terrifying message. Few phrases are more frightening to a woman than "You have breast cancer." The follow-up tests took place on May 13. We received the results several days later.

When we called our physician, he was totally booked but made room for us at the end of the day on May 17. Dr. Royal Dean is a throwback to the old time family physician. I don't know if he makes house calls, but I wouldn't be surprised. He called us on the phone just to let us know he was praying for us. He sits in the examination room and talks to you for as long as you need. There is never the attitude of "I need to get to my next patient" communicated by him. After meeting with him to go over the ultrasound results, the word "CANCER" was first mentioned. He had already called a surgeon to make an appointment for us. Amazingly, the surgeon had an opening the next day.

Dr. Kwanho Chong is a very small man with a great big heart. He is a brilliant surgeon and took a lot of time to explain the procedures we would be facing and the options available to us. His first course of action was to schedule a biopsy. The only opening the radiologist had available was on May 20, two days later. We scheduled the appointment.

The biopsy took place on a Thursday. We were told that the results could take three or four days before they would become available. Dr. Chong called the next day to let us know that he had received the results. When he called, though, we were not able to answer the phone. We returned his call, but his office had closed for the weekend. To go through the weekend without knowing the results was going to be very stressful, so we called his answering service, left our cell phone number, and asked him to call us back. Even though it was after hours and on a weekend, he called back about twenty minutes later. The tumor was malignant and needed to be removed.

You have cancer. Where do you go from there? You do the next thing.

Elisabeth Elliot had made that statement several years ago. She and her husband Jim were missionaries in Ecuador during the 1950's. Along with four other men, Jim was martyred by a tribe of Waodani. The pictures of their story were on the front cover of *Life* magazine and turned into a major motion picture, *End of the Spear*. As she went through the process of planning the funeral, keeping the ministry going, and raising a young daughter, Elisabeth was asked how she was able to get through that terrible ordeal. She simply replied, "I just do the next thing." That has become our motto in facing cancer. Don't get overwhelmed with the many events that you must deal with in the future. Do the next thing.

For us, the next step was to make another appointment with Dr. Chong and plan Nicki's surgery. He just happened to have an opening on Monday, May 24. We took the appointment.

Sunday, we told the people in our church. I stated the situation in a plain and simple manner. It was not a time for panic or fear; it was a time for faith, hope, and prayer. More than three hundred times in the Bible, God tells us to "fear not." The primary reason He tells us not to fear is because He is with us. We do not know the future, but we can have a personal relationship with the God who controls the future.

By divine coincidence, a community-wide prayer meeting was scheduled for that evening. Our community has a group of twenty to twenty-five pastors who meet every Wednesday at lunchtime to pray together. We pray for one another's ministries and families. We pray for our community and its leaders. The National Day of Prayer breakfast is planned by this group, as well as what have become known as "concerts of prayer." These are community-wide events scheduled twice a year. They are times of singing, self-examination, and prayer. I announced our situation at this meeting. The prayer teams had been unleashed.

Several years ago, a major medical school did a study on the effects of prayer and surgery. A large number of people facing surgery were identified as the study group and divided into two subgroups. Prayer groups were given the names of half of the individuals who would be facing surgery. Those being studied were not told what was taking place, so those being prayed for were unaware of that fact. The patients being prayed for had a much higher rate of successful surgery and a much faster recovery rate than did those who had no one praying for them.

Some might think this is just a coincidence. If so, we wanted to make sure that people prayed for us so that those coincidences would continue on our behalf. Our pastors' group prayed and encouraged their congregations to pray. Friends and families were praying and e-mailing our situation to those within their sphere of influence. We received notes from people we did not know who stated that they were praying for us.

On May 24, we met with Dr. Chong to map out our strategy. He described the options available to us and gave us the details on each option. The cancer was aggressive and growing quickly. We could do a mastectomy or a lumpectomy combined with radiation. After all the information was given to us, we decided on a lumpectomy. We made our decision based primarily on the fact that the cure rate for breast cancer does not increase with having the breast removed.

We still had many questions on the radiation treatment, so we asked Dr. Chong for a referral. Simi Valley Hospital has a good oncology department, and Dr. Victor Schweitzer was the radiation oncologist to whom we were referred. There was only one problem; he was leaving for vacation the next morning. He could see us either in a week or in the next hour.

We had a very good consultation with Dr. Schweitzer and had all of our questions answered. We called Dr. Chong to tell him of our decision to have the lumpectomy. He informed us that he had already scheduled the surgery for Wednesday, May 26. I don't know what the world record is for the fastest cancer treatment, but we went from detection to surgery in a matter of eight days.

There was no cancer discovered in the lymph nodes. Had we waited or had a doctor not been able to see us for a week, we do not know what the results would have been. We only know that in our case, speed mattered.

Chapter 4

God shows His presence in different ways. In many situations, He reveals Himself in little things. As Nicki was going through her biopsy, she was comforted by the words of Saint Paul in Philippians 4:13 NKJV, *"I can do all things through Christ who strengthens me."* As she was wheeled into the operating room, those same words filled her heart and her mind.

After the surgery was completed, Dr. Chong came out to give us the results. When he stated, "I think we got all of the cancer," cheers, hugs, and tears were evident everywhere. As he was walking back into the recovery room, one of the hospital employees approached me and asked if I was with Nicki Jackson. I answered that I was and was told that a floral arrangement was downstairs, but it was too heavy to carry upstairs. My father-in-law went with her to bring the arrangement upstairs. When he returned, we were all in shock. This arrangement must have cost several hundred dollars. It had a dozen long-stemmed roses, nearly as many lilies, and dozens of other types of flowers. On the arrangement was the name of the florist and a note that simply stated, "I can do all things through Christ who strengthens me." No identification was listed.

Over the years, we have received many anonymous gifts. Some of them were simple and inexpensive. A few were very expensive. All of them had some sort of identification. They might state, "From a friend," "From your secret sister," or "From someone who cares." Some were given to another person to give to us anonymously. Many were given through the church. None had ever come without some kind of identification. I asked my daughter to call the florist to see if she could discover the identity of the donor. Ashley returned and reported, "The florist stated that the individual said Nicki would know who they were from."

The Bible says, *"Do not neglect to show hospitality to strangers, for by this, some have entertained angels without knowing it"* (Hebrews 13:2 NASB). Could the flowers have been sent by a friend who just decided to spend a fortune and remain unknown? Maybe.

Could God have sent an angel to the florist shop to purchase an expensive arrangement with heaven's pocket change and leave the exact same message which Nicki had been meditating on as a note of encouragement? It wouldn't be the first time God moved in that way.

Chapter 5

My wife is a Certified Interior Designer in the state of California. She has worked on multi-million-dollar homes, churches, doctor's offices, and the information center of the Santa Monica Mountains Conservancy in Malibu. She also teaches interior design at a local college. Many years ago, she worked on a home in a very exclusive area of Los Angeles. She developed a good relationship with her client and ended up hiring her as an assistant in Nicki J Interiors. They became very good friends and later she became a member of our congregation.

After our first meeting with the surgeon, we returned home and listened to our voicemail. Nicki's assistant had called, and her message stated, "I don't know why this is happening. God must not be hearing my prayers." How many people have that same attitude? "If something bad happens, it must be because I don't pray well enough, or because God wants to punish me."

The causes of disease and illness are often a mystery. We know about germs, viruses, and bacteria. Why is it, though, that some get sick and some don't? Why does the drunk driver seem to survive the accident and the mother of two small children doesn't? The Bible calls these "mysteries." We do not know the answer to that question, and God has chosen to remain silent.

The best example of this is the Bible character Job. One of the richest and most righteous men in the area, Job lost everything in a day. Possessions, family, and health were all taken from him without any explanation. His friends stated that the problem must have been a secret sin in his life. His wife told him to "curse God and die." How would you like to come home to her every night?

The Bible claims that a spiritual battle between God and Satan was the cause of his problems, but Job never learned that. Most people believe that the theme to the book of Job is suffering. It isn't. The theme to the book of Job is that God has the right to do what He wants. Once Job learned that truth, life became bearable again.

How can that be? How can believing that God has the right to bring pain and sorrow into my life bring meaning into my existence? It works this way. When I accept God's right to run my life, I stop asking the "Why?" question and start asking the "Now what?" question. If I believe God owes me a life with few problems, I spend my whole life asking, "God, why did you do this to me? It's not fair."

Several years ago, my wife and I were browsing through a very upscale market in our community. As I walked past the meat counter, there was a roast in the window with a sticker price of $129.95 per pound. I'm always embarrassing my wife by asking dumb questions, but this one I couldn't ignore. I asked the butcher if the price was a mistake. He said that the roast was Kobe beef and was imported from Japan. When the calf is born, it is placed in a harness and fed a very special diet. Every day, women come in and massage the muscles of these animals. They are pampered like crazy. This process keeps the muscles from developing, making the meat very tender.

I meet people who believe they should be treated like Kobe beef. "Give me a life full of blessings and no trials." It sounds wonderful, except that no muscles are developed. God allows trials in our lives so that muscles develop. A friend told me, "When meat is placed in the pressure cooker, it becomes more tender."

When I begin to see my problems through the love of God, I understand that He will never allow anything that would be ultimately harmful to me. I then ask, "God I don't understand why you allowed this, but would you give me the strength to seek your guidance as I make my way through this trial?"

Before you contemplate all the complexities of that statement, let me remind you that this was exactly how Jesus lived out His life. The prophet Isaiah stated that the Messiah would be *"a man of sorrows and acquainted with grief"* (Isaiah 53:3 NASB). This is why Jesus prayed in the Garden of Gethsemane, *"Not my will but Thine be done"* (Luke 22:42 KJV). He was acknowledging God's right to bring pain into His life if it could accomplish God's will.

I will be honest with you. My family, friends, and church members hated this cancer. I did too! We all wanted it to go away. We prayed for God to touch us and to give us a divine healing. I know people who have seen God do extraordinary miracles in their lives. I believed God could do that in Nicki's life, and we were asking for Him to do just that. That was our will.

However, God seemed to have a different direction for us to follow. I can make up all sorts of "maybes" that God had in mind. They would all be guesses. Our purpose was to find God in the middle of our trial. He was with Daniel in the lion's den, with Joseph in the middle of his imprisonment, and with the apostles as they were persecuted by the Roman government. In the middle of their pain, they found God and rejoiced in their infirmity.

We did not know where this disease would lead, but we anticipated it would lead to recovery. We were confident, though, of only one reality. God had allowed this trial to come our way, and He would provide peace in the middle of the battle. *"I can do all things through Christ who strengthens me"* (Philippians 4:13 NKJV) works even for those who are going through cancer.

Chapter 6

Time.

It is the only commodity that everyone has in equal amounts. While we may live many more years until our deaths, we all have sixty minutes in an hour, twenty-four hours in a day, and three hundred and sixty-five days in a year.

When a premature death occurs, we feel ripped off because that individual didn't get to live out his or her seventy-five years; however, God never promised us tomorrow or next year. God only promised us today. That is why Jesus taught us in the Lord's Prayer to say, *"Give us this day our daily bread."* (Matthew 6:11 NASB)

Life is fragile, and life is temporary. None of us will leave this world alive. Regardless of all the incredible life-saving and life-prolonging discoveries that have taken place over the last few decades, the death rate has not changed. It is still one per person. Every one of us will one day be the focal point of a funeral.

Cancer reminds us of that fact. We want to plan our lives for every little contingency. We will go to college, get married, have three kids, buy a house in the suburbs, join a church and a country club, watch our kids graduate and get married, have kids of their own, retire, and enjoy being grandparents. One of these days, we will contemplate death, but that is for when we are old.

Our friends Joe and Joleen were the perfect couple. They were good-looking, popular, and intelligent. After they were married, Joe was transferred to Cleveland. It was a move up the corporate ladder, and it fit into their future plans. They had three children, joined a church, stayed in touch with friends and family, and lived out their life. They had it all.

They did not plan on their two-and-a-half-year-old daughter being diagnosed with leukemia. No longer were they making plans for retirement, next year's vacation, and the next step up the corporate ladder.

For two years, they just did the next thing. It can feel frustrating to live this way because we want to be in control of our future; however, God wants to be in control of our future. Diseases, accidents, and trials are all ways that God reminds us we are to live one day at a time.

Melissa finished all of her treatments, and it looks like a full recovery. It was a detour in their life and not a derailment. It taught them to live day to day. Joleen called us on the phone this week to let us know that Melissa and her sister Maegan just earned their black belts in Tae Kwon Do. Life goes on.

Chapter 7

It is known as the Bermuda Triangle. Planes and boats enter into its location and are never heard from again. It is scary. To many, the journey from cancer to wellness is like going through the Bermuda Triangle. It is uncharted territory and can be very scary.

One of the reasons cancer can be such a frightening experience is because no one is prepared to make the decisions that need to be made. Every time we turned around, someone was demanding that a decision be made. Where do you go to know what decisions are right? As we went through our journey, I began to write out decisions that we made right and decisions we might have done better. Out of this came a set of ten cardinal rules. You will need to develop your own, but hopefully, these will get you started in the right direction.

1. **Stay in control.** You need to be the final voice in deciding what will and will not be done. You will be surrounded by brilliant people who have gone through this before and who know what they are doing, but the final decision must always be yours. Don't allow yourself to be bullied.
2. **Don't be afraid to ask questions.** It doesn't always seem this way, but your medical team works for you. The fact that they know what they are doing means little if you are constantly having anxiety attacks because you fear the worst. You have not only hired them to heal your body, but you also need them to inform you of the whats and the whys so that your spirit can be at rest. Ask questions when

you don't know. This also gives you permission to seek second opinions. When in doubt, ask.

3. **Don't ask why—ask, "What now?"** Were God Himself to come down and explain why He allowed you to have a life-threatening disease, you would probably finish the conversation by saying, "But why me?" You will be better able to deal with your situation if you simply ask, "What now?" If you need a "God, I don't understand why this is happening" file, put it in your drawer and place all of your questions in it. Time often answers those questions, but it is more important in the present for you to deal with what is taking place than to question why it is occurring.

4. **Recognize that your condition will put you in a unique position to help others.** As you go through tests, surgery, consultations, chemotherapy, and radiation, the feeling often arises that the only one going through trials is you. However, many people are watching how you respond to each situation. You will give them hope, or you will bring discouragement to them by what you say and how you behave. Choose to give hope.

5. **Take your naps.** The world will continue to spin if you get off it for a short time. Rest is one of the most important "medicines" you will take. It is not superficial; it is essential. Take naps.

6. **Do not blame.** Blame causes you to focus on the past, which cannot be changed. Focus on the future. That is where you will live. You do want to live, don't you?

7. **Allow people to care for you.** Some dear friends decided to have a fundraiser for us at a local pizza parlor. I told my niece that we felt a little awkward about this attention. She replied, "It sounds like you are too proud to let people help." I hate it when people nail me to the wall. People want to help. Those who love you see this as an opportunity to minister to you. Let them.

8. **Develop a support group.** It could be people in your church, your neighbors, your friends from work, or a group recommended by your doctor. You need to be supported. You need help. Let them help you. It helps them, too.

9. **Be gracious to the stupid people in your world.** You will be shocked at the insensitivity of some people. Expect it, assume they are ignorant and not bad, and move on. Remember, rule #1 is "Stay in control." If you let others control you by reacting to everything they say, you will not be in control. Do not let thoughtless people control your life.
10. **Get through the bad days and enjoy the good days.** There will be plenty of bad days on your way to recovery. There is no good way to deal with those days other than to go through them. They do not stay forever. Get through them, because good days will come. Don't focus on the bad days; it will spoil the good ones. Endure the bad days, but enjoy the good ones. It will make your journey to wellness a little more hopeful.

Chapter 8

On July 17, 64 AD, Rome began to burn, and Nero watched. In 1871, Mrs. O'Leary's cow kicked over a lantern, and the Great Chicago Fire began. In 2004, a careless camper ignited the great Southern California fire. The entire mountain range between Simi Valley and Valencia went up in flames. Firefighters decided to let the mountains burn and save homes. If you were to drive around the exterior of Simi Valley, you would notice charred areas all the way up to the walls of people's back yards. The firefighters did an incredible job of allowing the grass to burn while saving every home in our city. They decided to allow the grass, shrubs, and trees to burn because they knew nature would cause everything to grow back.

I mentioned this in a sermon one Sunday, and a lady came up to me after the service to talk. Knowing that she was a science teacher, I was interested in whether I had gotten all of my facts right. She told me my comments were correct and then said that the process is called scarification and vernalization. It is the process by which nature replenishes itself after a raging fire. She then told me that there are some seeds that only crack open during a fire. In other words, without the fire, those seeds would never germinate and produce life. It is only in the fire that life can take place. What God wove into the world of nature is just as relevant for those of us living life.

There are some truths that can only be learned under what Peter called "fiery trials." I recently learned a new application for this truth. Several years ago, I came across a book by Rabbi Daniel Lapin entitled *Buried Treasure*. It is a study of Hebrew root words. Rabbi Lapin has since become one of my favorite writers. In his book, he stated that Hebrew is unlike any other language in its origin of root words. While English words can be understood through their root derivation, that is not necessarily true in every case. For instance, a runner who is fast has the exact opposite definition from a shirt that is colorfast. Hebrew words are different. If two Hebrew words have the same root, they have to have a similar definition.

My wife and I take classes periodically at the University of Judaism in Los Angeles. It keeps us fresh in the Old Testament, often gives us spiritual applications to our understanding of the New Testament, and opens up dialogue opportunities between Christians and Jews.

Not long ago, we attended a lecture by radio personality Dennis Prager. Dennis is a devout Jew with a good reputation around our nation who began about ten years ago to teach the Torah (the five books of Moses) verse by verse. Over the years, Dennis and I have interacted with each other on several occasions and have become casual friends. My schedule allows Nicki and me to attend his lectures about five or six times a year. On one occasion, he was teaching from Deuteronomy 15 on the importance of Jewish holidays. Several of the Jewish holidays were joyful events and did not require much effort; however, some of the holidays involved a great sacrifice of effort and expense. He then made the comment, "Did you know that the root word for *sacrifice* and the root word for *intimacy* are the same?" I am sure his statement passed over the heads of most of his listeners. It hit me right in the heart.

God allowed this fiery ordeal to invade our life. If I resent it and become bitter, it will drive a wedge between Nicki and me and between me and God. If we accept it as God's special gift, an opportunity to suffer, I will develop a greater intimacy with both my wife and my God.

Far from being morbid, it is common sense. One of the reasons we love our children so much is because of all the sacrifices we have made in raising them. That which we willingly suffer for is that which we will love most.

Chapter 9

The American Psychiatric Association lists hundreds of phobias. Some of them seem rather silly to the average person. Nephophobia is the fear of clouds, alliumphobia is the fear of garlic, sinistrophobia is the fear of left-handedness, erytophobia is the fear of red lights, homilophobia is the fear of sermons (what?), xanthophobia is the fear of yellow, and xylophobia is the fear of wood.

Pathophobia is the fear of disease. Fears of some illnesses, such as brain disease, nervous disorders, fevers, skin lesions, tetanus, and tuberculosis have their own names. At this point, cancer does not. I am surprised by that because one of the primary fears for women is breast cancer. Many women do not get mammograms simply because they fear being told that they have cancer. In this issue, ignorance is not bliss—it is deadly.

In the battle against cancer, overcoming our fears is a primary obstacle. We fear leaving our families, hospital stays, financial ruin, and dozens of other issues. At its heart, fear is a ruthless oppressor. Whatever we fear controls us. Nicki and I chose to hit this fear head-on.

In our first appointment with our surgeon Dr. Chong, he used various terms to describe the tumor. Each term was nice-sounding, but it skirted around the truth. Nicki finally said, "I have cancer; it is all right to say that word." Once you say the phrase "I have cancer," that fear is behind you. There will be other fears that must be defeated, but that one was behind us.

Several months ago, Dr. Phil McGraw was on a talk show. Dr. Phil became a household name several years ago because of his Tuesday visits with Oprah Winfrey. He currently hosts his own popular syndicated talk show. In addition, he is a successful author, lecturer, and father. Dr. Phil is a very interesting study in his own right. He is highly educated but is also filled with an incredible amount of common sense and keen insight. I do not know his spiritual beliefs, but much of his counsel is consistent with what the Bible teaches.

As he was being interviewed, a woman called and mentioned a fear she was facing. Dr. Phil made one of those clarifying statements which caused the light bulb to turn on in my mind. Dr. Phil stated, "There are not many fears; there is really only one, the fear of losing control." The reason people fear germs, the outdoors, elevators, flies, diseases, and a hundred other things is because they feel they have lost control of their situation.

In our battle with cancer, we made the commitment that we would be the deciding factor in any decisions made. Some of the medical people we have worked with have encouraged that. Others have resented our intrusion into their domain. We have also learned that, even though we will make all final decisions, we are not in control. We have no control over the cancer cells, the dates of tests, which technicians will be available, how the insurance company will respond, whether the chemotherapy will be successful, and a dozen other situations. This is why so many people fear cancer; they understand that, as patients, they can only respond to the cancer, not control it.

This is where the Bible and Dr. Phil intersect. Dr. Phil was right in his assessment of fear. There is only one fear, the fear of not being in control, and that fear can be oppressive. There is one exception. The Bible calls it "the fear of the Lord." The Bible states, *"In the fear of the Lord there is strong confidence…in the fear of the Lord is a fountain of life…the fear of the Lord is the beginning of wisdom"* (Proverbs 14:26, 27; 9:10 NASB).

The fear of the Lord is the understanding that God is in control, oversees our thoughts and actions, and will hold us accountable. Those who live their lives in the fear of the Lord recognize they are not in control of the situation. We can't control the cars coming in the opposite direction, the gang members across town, or the airplane we will be using next week. Rather than cause us to panic, the fear of the Lord frees us because we understand that, while we cannot be in control of our circumstances, God is.

When we live our lives understanding that God is in control of our situation, even tragedies can result in peace and security.

This is one of the great paradoxes in the Bible. I wrote earlier that fear is a paralyzing emotion. The fear of the Lord, however, is a very liberating belief. In the Bible, the phrase *fear not* appears 365 times. That is one time for every day of the year. It usually appears with the additional comment, "for I am with you." When we walk in the fear of the Lord, we do not need to fear anything else.

We do not fear cancer; we fear the Lord, and we understand that He has allowed this situation in our life for a reason. We have not asked why; we have asked, "What now?" and we know that God has a great final chapter planned for our life.

Recognizing that what we fear controls us, we have chosen to fear God. His control over our life has resulted in peace.

Chapter 10

How would *60 Minutes* handle interviewing God? If they represented the public at large, the first question asked would be, "Why do you allow suffering in the world?" I don't know of anyone who has not asked that question at least once. Theologians have debated it for thousands of years. The Bible is not silent on the suffering of godly people. The children of Israel were in slavery for four hundred years before God sent Moses to deliver them. When Jesus was born, King Herod sent his soldiers to kill all of the children of Bethlehem two years old and under. The Westminster Catechism states that Jesus "suffered under Pontius Pilate." God is not unsympathetic to the suffering of the human race.

We are told in the Bible that the problem of suffering came into the world because of man's rebellion against God's plan. However, God has chosen not to reveal His "why". He did something better: He revealed what can happen if we use our suffering to bring glory to Him. The apostle Paul wrote,

> "Blessed be the God and Father of our Lord Jesus Christ, the Father of mercies and God of all comfort, who comforts us in all our affliction so that we will be able to comfort those who are in any affliction with the comfort with which we ourselves are comforted by God. For just as the sufferings of Christ are ours in abundance, so also our comfort is abundant through Christ. But if we are afflicted, it is for your comfort and salvation; or if we are comforted, it is for your comfort, which is effective in the patient, enduring of the same sufferings which we also suffer; and our hope for you is firmly

> *grounded, knowing that as you are sharers of our sufferings, so also you are sharers of our comfort"*(2 Corinthians 1:3-7 NASB).

In this passage, Paul states at least four important facts about God and suffering that are important to know.

First, God is the originator of comfort and mercy. The Greeks and the Romans believed that the gods were too busy to care for the human race. The Hebrew and Christian God brought compassion into the world. This is why both the Old and New Testaments are filled with passages dealing with our responsibility to take care of widows, orphans, the ill, and the infirm. Because of sin, God could not eliminate suffering, so He decided to overcome it with His mercy.

Second, God offers comfort to those who are suffering. When I was in high school, I learned to play pinochle. It is a card game and has what are known as trump cards. Once the trump suit is called, any card in that suit is a trump card. A nine of the trump suit is higher than an ace of another suit. God could not cancel suffering, so He manifests His mercy and trumps it.

When God's comfort is given to us, we are not obligated to accept it. We can reject His mercy, and we can reject Him. However, the suffering continues. As we were going through the suffering of treatments, aftermath of treatments, and insurance companies, we sought His comfort. He always came through.

Third, God uses our comfort to help others who are suffering. As we faced Nicki's surgery, she felt very restless. One of her clients had been diagnosed with breast cancer several years ago and was in remission. Nicki decided to call her on the phone to seek counsel. She and Annette talked for several hours. At the conclusion of their conversation, Nicki was greatly encouraged and it helped bring peace for her upcoming surgery.

God does not make us suffer so we can help others. All of us suffer to some degree or another. God simply uses that suffering as a platform to help others going through the same struggles.

Chuck Colson was known during the Watergate scandal as "President Nixon's hatchet man." Through his involvement in the cover-up, he spent several years in a federal penitentiary. I don't know if he would have been able to bring comfort to Nicki as she faced her cancer surgery. I do know that his "Prison Fellowship" is the most effective organization in our nation in ministering to prisoners and their families. That is because Chuck Colson was there and he understood their unique struggles. He was able to comfort them because he was comforted by others.

Fourth, God uses suffering to develop character in our lives. Paul mentions patience and hope in the passage, but compassion, endurance, and intimacy with God can also be developed through suffering. What parent is not drawn closer to a child who has to go in for surgery? Children are often brought closer to their parents after Mom or Dad has a stroke or heart attack. The suffering that one experiences is an opportunity for others to step in and lend a hand. That draws people closer together.

Your pain might not be from cancer. It may be another disease. It might be the loss of a limb or one of the five senses. Maybe one of your parents died. It may be that you never knew your parents. Maybe you were abused or molested as a child. Pain and suffering come in many different sizes and colors. There is a corresponding color of God's mercy for whatever suffering you experience. Reach out and grab it. It will get you through the fiery trials of life.

Chapter 11

It is known as the Lazarus syndrome. It is the process by which medical personnel come to believe that they have the power to heal. It is based on the story in the Bible where Jesus raised Lazarus from the dead.

Because of the extraordinary skills of so many in the medical field, it is very easy to understand how this attitude can develop. If asked, most medical personnel would not admit to having this attitude. Many do not. However, it can become noticeable as you make your way through the labyrinth of options and decisions that have to be made. Here is what we have learned in this journey to wellness.

First, most medical personnel are kind, compassionate people who are in medicine because they care about people and gain a great satisfaction from seeing people regain their health. We have been incredibly fortunate in the individuals we have worked with. The number of doctors, nurses, and technicians who went out of their way to accommodate our schedule was countless. We are so grateful for each of them.

It is very easy to take for granted those who serve you through their medical expertise. They are also human and can have their feelings hurt. We have found that the best way to keep those in the medical field on your side is to treat them with respect.

Second, the medical personnel know more about cancer than we do. Those who minister to you have dedicated their lives to understanding everything there is to know about the disease for which you are seeking treatment. They are an incredible resource.

One of the many frustrations people have who are going through any potentially fatal disease is the incredible number of different opinions that are out there. One voice tells you to take vitamins and drink juices. The next one tells you that radical surgery is the only way to be safe. Another voice recommends that you use modern technology. Whom do you listen to?

We made the decision to limit the number of people to whom we would listen. There is always one more opinion out there, which will throw you into complete confusion. Pick out a few experts, and don't be afraid to tactfully challenge their conclusions while at the same time respecting their knowledge. Remember, you may need to come back for their skills, so don't burn your bridges.

Third, knowing they know more, they will try to steer you in the way they think is best. Because they are skilled, they believe their way is right. That is because they have seen so many patients succeed under their care. Begin with the assumption that they want you to get well. Doing that will make any disagreement you have easier to deal with. They know more and have been down this road before. Don't be threatened by that.

While they have a far greater understanding of your disease than you do, they are influenced by outside forces as you are. Schedules, insurance companies, peers, and educational background all go into their decision-making process. They know more, but do not know all.

Fourth, you need to stay in control. While you know less about cancer than anyone else in the room, it is your life, and you need to stay in control. There is one thing you know better than anyone else: how you feel. Don't be afraid to share that.

This is not to say that you should make dumb decisions just to let them know you are the boss. A dumb decision can cost you your life, so don't play "king of the hill" just to prove a point. If you don't know about a situation or are unsure of what is best, ask for their recommendation. "What would you do in my situation?" is always an acceptable question.

If you find that you are being bullied by a doctor, nurse, or practice, it is your right to find another doctor. It is your body, and it is your life. Be humble, ask lots of questions, and don't be afraid to get a second opinion. When in doubt, yield to the doctor's expertise, but always be the one to make the decision. If you really can't make a decision, delegate it to someone you trust, but understand it is your decision.

Stay in control.

Chapter 12

Military experts tell us that one of the greatest forms of punishment is isolation. This is why prisons use an isolation chamber to break their worst inmates. Man was not created to live alone. Common sense confirms this to be true. As our nation grew and expanded, most Americans lived within a day's journey of most of their family members. A majority of Americans even lived in the same city as their parents and siblings. My wife grew up living next door to her grandparents.

That all changed after World War II. Suddenly, the West Coast saw an influx of GIs coming home from the Pacific, landing at a West Coast port, and going no farther. The interstate highway came into being in the early 1950's. Airplane travel became more economical and safer, allowing people to live in one area and visit relatives in another. Large corporations began transferring employees around the nation. The standing joke at IBM was that it stood for "I've Been Moved."

This made the middle class in America larger, but it also placed a new burden on the American family. For the first time, children were growing up with no grandparents, aunts, uncles, and cousins in their immediate vicinity. Families moved into new neighborhoods, made new friends, joined churches and service clubs, and replaced the extended family with alternatives.

Then came the 1960's and 70's. Divorce, apartment complexes, job transfers, and moving up the social ladder all resulted in our society going through an incredible change. People no longer knew the people living around them. Technology only increased this isolation. Air conditioning allowed people to stay inside instead of sitting on the porch and talking to people who walked by. Television allowed people to be entertained without going to the town square. Movies-on-Demand, VCRs, and DVDs made it possible for people to see movies without going to the theater. The Internet has now freed people from actually talking to each other. We can now just type in a note and punch a button. Social media makes it possible to become anonymously intimate with people we have never met.

Let me add that this technology has also kept families and friends together who are separated by the miles. I am not criticizing the advances, only showing how they have allowed people to become isolated. In our city, 30 percent of our homes have new residents each year. Why get to know your neighbors if they are going to move in a year? That feeds into the isolation.

This has resulted in disastrous consequences. In Southern California, a third of the population belongs to no organization. That means that there are millions of people who are not in the Rotary, a bowling league, Little League, church, or PTA. It is unlikely that they know their neighbors well, if at all. What happens when they lose their jobs, have financial setbacks, or develop cancer? There is no support group to hold them up.

The Bible stresses the value of support groups. The word used is *fellowship*. It is one of the most important words in the Bible. We read, *"They were continually devoting themselves to the apostles' teaching, and to fellowship, to the breaking of bread and to prayer…and all those who had believed were together, and had all things in common; and they began selling their property and possessions, and were sharing them with all, as anyone might have need"* (Acts 2:42, 44, 45 NASB).

That is a support group. We have such a support group. It includes family, church, and friends. We have invested in the lives of hundreds over the years, and that investment came back with interest during our battle with cancer.

We received the following letter from a member of our support group. She wrote,

> Pastor Glen and Nicki,
> You've always bathed us in prayer, so now, we're bathing you in prayer. May you know how much your church family loves you; you mean the world to us. You're part of our

family. And we know that God loves you even more than we do. So with these words, be reminded; When you can't trace His hand, trust His heart. We will be there for you.

> The Lord bless and keep you,
> The ---- family
> XOXO

That letter could have been written by one of dozens of people. To keep people informed, we set up a friends and family e-mail list. By writing one letter, we kept everyone informed. We probably had over a hundred people on our address list. When I brought Nicki home from the hospital after her porta-cath was installed, I sent a two-sentence note to our list just to keep them updated. We received close to twenty-five replies to my note. Most of the replies were one-sentence notes of prayer and encouragement. They were all meaningful.

There are support groups available for just about any situation. However, if you wait until help is needed before joining a group, you limit the number of people available. Begin today to build your resources. Find a church that meets your needs. Join a social club. Pick out a hobby you can do with others. Become involved in your neighborhood. If you have children, join the PTA and get your children involved in church and school activities. (Don't over-commit them. Remember, they need rest, too).

Chapter 12b

I would not be in the ministry today if it were not for Dean and Joetta Milsap. When I committed my life to full-time ministry, they were my spiritual adopted parents. They took me, as a young man, under their wings and taught me how to love people, how to minister to the needs of others, and how to serve God's people. After Nicki and I moved to Simi Valley, Joetta was diagnosed with a brain tumor, went into a coma, and eventually passed away.

Because of the distance, we were out of the loop and didn't know what was taking place. Several times a week, I called to get an update on Joetta's condition and to pray for Dean and his two children. I got an answering machine and never did talk to a real person until after Joetta passed away.

How do you communicate with the many people who want to know how you are feeling and who want to talk to you when you don't feel like talking to anyone? Many people create a group on Facebook which is very public. The answer came to me through our friends Joe and Joleen. Joleen received a note informing her that an acquaintance had been diagnosed with breast cancer and donations were being accepted. A website was listed to which people could log on for more information. Some people set up a blog to keep friends updated.

The internet and social media is ideal in keeping people informed about your situation and allowing them to send notes back to you.

All of us have friends around us who would be honored to post or blog for you if you were diagnosed with a serious illness. Designate a person to keep up the site each day. It would keep your friends informed, give them an outlet for concern, and encourage you with the many expressions of love

As Martha Stewart says, "It's a good thing."

Chapter 13

As we went through the process of battling cancer, one of the benefits we enjoyed was the number of people who wanted to bring us meals. Most churches have a lot of good cooks. Ours is no exception.

Over the years, we have taken hundreds of meals to those who were sick, had a baby, lost a loved one, or were just tired. It is one of the joys of being in the ministry. When people found out that we were facing cancer, we had people standing in line to bring in meals. Most of them were tasty. Here are some suggestions we learned for handling this blessing.

First, designate one individual to coordinate the meals. Most churches already have a system to provide for this. You can also set up a meal organizer web site. If this isn't assigned, you will have a dozen gigantic dinners the first night you come home.

Second, find out any restrictions on diet and taste. Try to remember that you are cooking for them, not you. If they don't like chicken, don't make your favorite chicken recipe. You don't need to impress them with your culinary skills; just keep it simple.

Third, don't be afraid to bring something for the freezer. Pasta sauce, meatloaf, and casseroles can all be put into containers that go from freezer to oven. Remember to put the cooking instructions on a three-by-five card and bring it in a throw-away container. This way, they don't have to wash and return it. Make things easy on them. Sealed bags of lettuce for salads are very convenient, and bottled dressings can be included at the same time. Cut-up fruit makes a wonderful dessert and is low-fat, low-calorie, and delicious.

Fourth, if you can't cook, don't. Pay to have a pizza delivered. Pick up Chinese takeout. Go to Costco, Marie Callender's, Boston Market, or any of a dozen other food establishments and bring in a prepared delicious meal.

Fifth, don't experiment on them. Don't try a new recipe to see if it's any good. Also, cook the food the way they like it. Remember, you are seeking to be a blessing to them. If they don't like certain items, accommodate them. You don't bless them by cooking food in a way they find distasteful. If they have simple tastes or don't like certain types of food, this is not the time to try to reform them.

Sixth, work within their schedule, not yours. If the husband doesn't get home from work until seven-thirty, don't bring dinner at five p.m. If the wife has a night job beginning at six p.m., don't deliver dinner at six-thirty. If your schedule for delivery doesn't mesh with their dinner time, be creative. Fix a casserole with oven instructions. Bring rolls and cold cuts that can be put in the refrigerator. Provide soup in a container that can be warmed up. Just remember that your desire should be to make life easier for them.

Seventh, remember the children. Children eat differently than do adults. Don't be afraid to include something that is specifically designed for the kids. Cookies, frozen yogurt, Jell-O, or their favorite fruit are all acceptable. Throw in a kid's toy. Parents will appreciate it.

Chapter 14

We all have friends who know someone who had a serious illness, found the magic pill, and feel you should try their remedy. Some are devoted to a spiritual solution and avoid all medical solutions. Others have heard of a clinic somewhere. Some know of a supplement that works wonders. Most people are committed to a traditional medical treatment regimen.

When those words "You have cancer" are uttered, the first question most people ask is, "What do I do now?" At our first meeting with our first doctor, Nicki stated, "I want to live. What do I need to do?" We then mapped out a plan we felt was best for us. When we didn't understand, we asked questions. When we felt uneasy, we sought a second opinion. When we felt ignorant, we read books.

Reading is a wonderful way to become informed. Many don't read as much as they should because they don't feel they have the time. One thing you have when you are battling cancer is time. We spent a lot of time in waiting rooms, hospitals, and doctor's offices. It gives you plenty of time to read. However, you must read wisely. Our country prints a thousand new books every day. You can't read them all. Therefore, you must use discretion in what you do read. Here are some suggestions.

First, do not read every book someone gives you. The individual who shares a book with you does so because they care about you. Accept it in that spirit. You are not obligated, however, to read it.

Second, scan the chapters. Begin with the index and see if there is a chapter that sounds interesting. Turn to that chapter and skim through the pages. If it shows possibilities, find a second chapter and repeat the process.

If you are still interested, read the book. Remember, you are not reading a novel; you are reading a research manual. You don't have to read the entire book to receive benefit from its pages. If only one chapter gives you good information, you can consider yourself blessed and skip the rest of the book.

Third, ask your medical personnel for book recommendations. They have been through this before and know the field. Here is a key to this: don't read books you don't understand. If your doctor recommends a book that is a bunch of medical jargon, it will do you no good if you don't understand what the author is saying. Rule of thumb on any book: anyone can complicate an issue. You are reading to gain clarity. If you read a few pages and it sounds like nonsense, move on to the next book. You are too busy to try to read something that makes no sense. Move on.

Fourth, use the Internet. The amount of information that one can gain from using a search engine is close to unlimited. As with books, there are good sites and there are bad sites. Many offer miracle cures for the right price. You need to avoid those. The answer to how you find a good website is the same as finding a good book. Much of it is trial and error. Find a site, read some basic information, and ask yourself some questions.

> Are their promises too good to be true?
> Do they seem to be too interested in finances?
> Are their stories verifiable?
> How does the medical community view them?
> Do their claims defy common sense?
> Has anyone you know used their product or system?

Fifth, don't be afraid of an off-the-wall book. You may not buy into the author's premise, but one chapter or one sentence may be of great help. No cure is ever accepted from day one, so don't write off something just because it is new. On the other hand, if no one accepts the author's claims, there may be a reason.

Sixth, let common sense be the deciding factor. Dennis Prager has a philosophy that makes a lot of sense. He states, "If I hear of a survey that just violates common sense, I know there is something wrong with the survey."

That attitude came to him after lecturing around the world and writing several books. He would hear of a survey that just sounded ridiculous but had the backing of some major organization. He thought that maybe he was wrong. However, the next survey would come out and have a totally different conclusion. He finally came to the conclusion that surveys are often taken by individuals or organizations with agendas to prove and very little common sense. Mr. Prager decided to ignore any survey that defied common sense, and he has never been wrong.

The same can be said for medical issues. If a diagnosis, cure, or disease sounds so bizarre as to defy common sense, it may be you that is in the right. Seek another opinion.

Chapter 15

Nurse Ratched. Jack Nicholson tormented her in the movie *One Flew Over the Cuckoo's Nest.* To everyone at the asylum, she was the nurse from hell. We have all had to deal with them, but going through a serious illness is not the time frame we wish to face her.

Annie Sullivan, Florence Nightingale, and Clara Barton were teachers and nurses who dedicated their lives to ministering to those going through extreme medical hardships. Even mean and nasty patients were treated with love and respect.

We have met all sorts of people in our walk through this valley. We dealt with one nurse who gave us an opportunity to experience stress and frustration. She was nowhere near Nurse Ratched, but we felt she lacked much of the compassion one usually associates with a nurse. She was very professional and informed in her field, but we had a hard time at first relating to her on a personal level.

When we met with our surgeon, he recommended an oncologist who practiced in our area. We met with her and decided to stick with her.

We also made the decision to seek a second opinion. Nicki is a highly respected Certified Interior Designer and has many doctors as clients. One client is well connected at both USC and UCLA medical schools. He gave us the name of a gifted oncologist who was willing to give us a second opinion. It was a wise decision on our part.

When we met with Dr. Chawla, he told us that our oncologist had made the right diagnosis and we were in good hands. He also suggested that we get a PET scan to have a basis of comparison when we were finished.

We called our oncologist and talked to the nurse. She told us that she would schedule a PET scan, but we really didn't need one. We checked with several other medical experts and ended up having the PET scan. However, we felt that her attitude came across as dismissive and condescending.

There are many ways of administering chemotherapy. Nicki needed to use the IV method. It was decided that the veins in her hands were not large enough, so a port-a-cath would need to be installed. This required going back to Dr. Chong, who performed the surgical procedure. A port-a-cath is about the size of a large button and is inserted in the fat tissue of the upper chest. It has a hole in it that is attached to a long tube. During surgery, the tube is installed into a large vein in the shoulder and runs all the way into the heart chamber. The "button" is then placed in the fat tissue, the skin is placed back over the unit, and the area heals up. When the IV treatment occurs, the needle is inserted into the "button," and the nurse does not need to find a receptive vein.

In explaining the procedure, the nurse told Nicki that the procedure was "no big deal." My wife has a mitral valve prolapse, which means a floppy heart valve. It is not life-threatening but can cause periodic palpitations. After this surgical procedure, she began to feel a slight discomfort in her chest. In addition, when Nicki came home after her surgery, the bruise from inserting her port-a-cath was very large. It was a big deal to us.

Dealing with doctors and nurses can be a tricky issue. Most of them are very professional and knowledgeable. Our nurse was very competent. However, her "no big deal" attitude left us with a negative feeling toward her. Any surgery is a big deal to the one going through it.

Many medical professionals understandably try to emotionally disassociate themselves from their patients for fear of losing one. That may be helpful for the medical personnel, but it is damaging to the patient's emotional well-being.

We solved this problem in two ways. First, we talked to her. When we went in for our chemotherapy instruction, we explained how we felt and what we wanted from her. We explained that having a port-a-cath surgically installed was a big deal to us. We needed her expertise, but Nicki needed to have people around her with positive attitudes and compassion. She responded in a positive way. She was apologetic and couldn't have been nicer. We see her periodically in public and always have a pleasant conversation. She learned a good lesson, too.

Second, we sought to be a positive influence to her. Many of the medical personnel who send out negative waves are unaware of how they are perceived by their patients. Simply telling them so with a positive attitude can work wonders.

There is actually a third way we dealt with our nurse. We prayed for her. When you pray for people, it changes them, and it changes how you think about them.

Let me tell you about a "Florence Nightingale." Before starting her chemotherapy, Nicki went in for a PET scan. The nurses were angels. They smiled, talked confidently to us, asked if they could get us anything, and explained everything that was going to take place. Thank you, Joan!

Thank you, Cindy, for responding to our comments and becoming an angel of mercy.

Chapter 16

What is it about people saying, "It's no big deal"? I mentioned this previously when the oncology nurse discussed the insertion of a port-a-cath. While there were no complications, it was a big deal for us.

The last step in Nicki's treatment was to have her port-a-cath removed. When Nicki's tests all came back with positive results, we made an appointment with Dr. Chong for this minor surgery. In discussing the procedure, Dr. Chong explained that any danger with the port-a-cath comes with the insertion. Taking it out is "no big deal." He actually used the exact same phrase as had our nurse. It must be taught in medical school.

So much for "It's no big deal." The anesthesiologist wrapped the blood pressure device too tight and gave Nicki a massive bruise on her arm. Nicki then had an allergic reaction to the bandage, causing several blisters to form on her chest. The bruise healed, the bandage was replaced, and healing did take place. However, it did become a big deal. We also learned that paper tape has a much lower instance of reaction than does the regular tape. It is your prerogative to ask for the medical team to use the paper tape. They probably won't do it if you don't ask. Cardinal rule #2 states, "Don't be afraid to ask questions." It never hurts to ask. It may save you from an allergic reaction.

This was just a reminder that there is no such thing as minor surgery. While the medical team may view your procedure as routine, there is always a possibility of problems.

Chapter 17

Narcissism is the belief that the world revolves around you. Even the most caring and giving people can become a little narcissistic in their battle with a potentially terminal disease. They don't feel well, can't get things for themselves, and need people to take care of their every need. For a period of time, it is both understandable and expected. However, this can also damage the relationships between the ones who are sick and those who care for them.

One of the most serious points of contention is resting. It is easy to understand why those battling cancer need rest. They may have just had surgery, didn't rest well the night before, have discomfort because of installed devices, or a dozen other reasons. They need to rest. If medication is necessary to receive the proper rest, then take the medication. A rested body is much better suited to recover from surgery.

However, there are others who also need rest. If your mate, friend, or family member is your primary caregiver, that person needs rest, also. When someone is sick and needs attention in the middle of the night, someone has to get up to give the attention. When one partner doesn't sleep well, the other often sleeps restlessly. We recognize that the one with the illness needs rest; we need to recognize that caregivers also need rest.

A noon nap, a quick rest when the caregiver gets home, or an early-to-bed scenario is not out of line.

Here is where the contention comes in. If you have stayed home and rested all day, you can hardly wait for Mr., Mrs., or Miss Wonderful to walk through the door so that you can talk to someone. On the other hand, that person had a poor night's sleep and a rough day at the office and can hardly wait to get home and take a nap.

One of the greatest causes of marital conflict is unfulfilled expectations. This is an unfulfilled expectation moment waiting to happen. This is why communication is so essential. This is also where a gracious spirit makes a big difference. Couples (or families) need to learn to read each other and act accordingly. It may be that the cancer patient is just seeking a little attention and a ten-minute talk would be a blessing. The other person can then have a short nap. On the other hand, it may be that the caretaker is so exhausted that he or she is going to fall asleep in the middle of the conversation. The best solution is to take a short nap and then talk. The key to solving this potential problem is to talk about it before it happens so that you can understand each other's position.

Here is the no-no. Neither partner can demand to get his or her way all the time. There needs to be sacrifice on both sides. When an illness like cancer strikes, both partners suffer. They have different roles, but both suffer, and both must give in so that the healing can take place. The result of one party always getting his or her way is the alienation of the other party.

Chapter 18

My wife is a strange creature. She expects me to give her eye contact when I talk to her. When I walk into the house with earbuds in my ears and my attention elsewhere, she doesn't like it. She even wants me to look at her during the middle of the ball game on television.

In the last chapter, I mentioned the importance of individuals battling a serious illness giving their caretakers permission to rest. In this chapter, I want to address the other side of that equation. The ones recovering from illness need attention. I don't mean that they need someone to be available to get them a drink of water. I mean they need to be the focal point of their lovers' attention. That means the paper goes down, the television gets turned off, and the neighbors don't count.

You look into each other's eyes and talk. This can drive men crazy because we don't know what to talk about. Then listen. If possible, go for a short walk and talk about the kids, the house, the events coming up, the Lakers. Hold hands, sing, read poetry, etc. The purpose is to make the other person aware that he or she is the center of your universe. The key to this is to make the person aware. If the other person doesn't know it, it hasn't happened.

The only way that happens is to give up something of value so that you can spend time with him or her. That makes the other person valuable. Your buddies, the newest movie opening, those free tickets all pale in comparison.

P.S. This works for people who are not battling disease, too.

Chapter 19

It is all right to cry. I state that on a pretty reliable source. Jesus cried. The apostles shed tears. Those going through cancer will cry, often. Nicki cried when she found out she had a tumor. She cried when she told others. She cried when she didn't want to. She cried when she was happy, and she cried when she was sad.

None of her tears were "woe is me" sobs. She cried over the thought of not seeing our daughters walk down the aisle, about leaving her parents, and about loving me. She was courageous when she needed to be, clear-headed when discussing various issues with our medical team, and truthful when discussing her situation with others.

Humans cry for all sorts of reasons. We cry at the birth of a baby and the death of a loved one. We cry when our team wins and when it loses. We cry mostly because God gave us the ability to shed tears. It is an emotional response to great joy and terrible pain, and God understands our tears. The psalmist wrote, "Weeping may last for the night, but a shout of joy comes in the morning."

Tears are a normal response to the issues of life. Don't apologize, and don't feel embarrassed; just let the tears flow. You'll feel better.

Chapter 20

The Mayo Clinic, Walter Reed, Johns Hopkins, and City of Hope are probably the most well-known hospitals in the United States. The most unusual health care facility in the nation is the Gesundheit Institute, located in the rolling hills of the Appalachian Mountains. The clinic and its founder, Hunter Adams, were made known to the world in the movie *Patch Adams*. The clinic does not charge for its services and carries no malpractice insurance. That is a pretty radical approach to the healing art. What is the key to their success? They combine modern medicine with laughter. They play practical jokes, dress up as clowns, and laugh.

I do not know Dr. Adams' spiritual beliefs, but I know that he has landed on a Biblical principle. The Bible states, *"A merry heart doeth good like a medicine"* (Proverbs 17:22 KJV). In other words, as *Reader's Digest* has stated for years, "Laughter is the best medicine."

The primary reason medical personnel do not involve themselves in treatment such as Patch Adams' is because disassociation makes it easier to make tough medical solutions. The liability is that patients are treated as objects and that creates tension, which harms the healing process.

We made the decision to laugh. Some of our humor was probably seen by others as bizarre. Some people might even see it as sick humor. It may have been, but those situations we did not share with others. While Nicki still had her hair, we went looking for hats and scarves. We chuckled as to what she would look like. Should she go for the Yul Brynner look, or the Susan Powter look? I stated that I was going to have my head shaved too. She didn't laugh at that. She didn't mind me looking silly but didn't think

I should look ridiculous. I thought about buying "Conehead caps" from the old *Saturday Night Live* skits, but thought better of it.

There is a fine line between laughing at the silly and mocking the one who is dealing with a situation. The one who has the medical problem is the one who has to set the guidelines. If you aren't sure, hold up. Here are some principles to guide you.

1. You have to earn the right to laugh at someone in public. Just because you know who someone is doesn't give you the right to laugh at them.
2. When in doubt, ask them privately. This will help you discern what their standards are.
3. Tears do not always communicate anger or resentment. Those going through cancer tend to have radical mood swings. Their tears may be an emotional release that brings about a laugh.
4. Ask forgiveness if your words turn out to be harmful. What is funny on one day may be resented the next. If you try to be funny and bomb, say "I'm sorry."
5. Never say something to be funny when you are angry. It will probably come out wrong and be seen as vindictive.

Learn to laugh. Even when you are facing a serious illness, "A merry heart doeth well, like a medicine." Laughter does make the road much easier to travel.

Chapter 21

I love studying the root meanings of words. I mentioned earlier the book *Buried Treasure* by Rabbi Daniel Lapin. It is nothing more than the meaning and significance of Hebrew words in the Old Testament. The New Testament was written in Greek and has its share of significant word studies. One of the most important words in the New Testament is *ecclesia*. It is usually translated *fellowship*.

We tend to think of fellowship as pizza and Coke at a Super Bowl party, a potluck dinner, or stopping at Starbucks for a café latte with some friends. *Ecclesia* often revolved around a meal, but the heart of its implementation was the sharing of needs and the ministering to those who were hurting.

In today's lingo, it would be a support group. However, it goes much deeper than most support groups might go. In many support groups of our time, the emphasis is on talking and sharing your feelings. In other words, go so you can get something off your chest. The healing process begins with talking, but that is not sufficient.

The true purpose of an effective support group is to allow people not just to get things off their chests, but to find healing. By venting or by expressing our anger, we may feel better, but we may not experience long-term healing. Talking begins the process, because that is how the true injuries are discovered. You then must find those injuries, determine a course of action, and let the healing begin.

One of the reasons many support groups have little long-term effectiveness is because they are not willing to go beyond how one feels to how things really are. Feelings are very important, but they do not always reflect things as they really are. The purpose of a support group is to find those feelings and base them within the context of reality. That helps people get their feelings under control and might actually help them to understand that their feelings are often based on incomplete and sometimes even wrong information.

Nicki decided to join a support group. At first, I didn't think it was necessary. Then, over coffee, I made an incredible discovery. She had some feelings going on inside her that I could not understand.

Boy, does that make you feel helpless. As we were discussing her joining a support group, I stated that I thought that our discussions were going fine. She made an off-the-wall comment that opened my eyes. She made a statement like, "I just don't feel supported around the house." I responded by saying, "I help around the house." She answered by saying, "See, that is why I need a support group."

It suddenly struck me what she was saying. She didn't need a support group to uncover deep and hidden hurts. She needed a support group where she could vent without those listening becoming defensive and saying, "Yes, we do." In the process of meeting with her support group, she could say things like, "Nobody loves me," "I feel unappreciated," "People don't care about me," and "People wouldn't even know if I were dead" without hurting people's feelings. Her support group could then help her understand what was happening and how to deal with her moods and emotions. She is loved, appreciated, and needed. She knew that. However, she needed to be reminded of that by an outside source.

Let me also say that there are support groups that can create major problems. Here is the best way I know how to tell the difference between a good one and a dangerous one. A good support group's primary task is to help you understand and deal with the struggles you are going through. In other words, their goal is to help you get well. A dangerous support group seeks to understand why you feel angry, hostile, bitter, or hurt; they encourage you to blame the other person and then allow you to stay in those feelings.

Your goal is not to learn how to stew in your pain and hurt; it is to get well.

Chapter 22

Boy, can I be dumb. I don't try to be; it just comes naturally. I think it is woven into my DNA.

Nicki and I came home from a weekend family reunion and began preparing for her first chemotherapy session on Wednesday. Her appointment was scheduled for nine a.m. and was to last about two hours.

I mentioned earlier a group of pastors who pray for and with each other. We meet at noon every Wednesday. Upon discovering that we would be home from her chemo treatment about eleven-thirty a.m. on Wednesday, I made preparations for my daughter to come home for her lunch break at noon to watch Nicki while I went to the prayer meeting.

Did I say that I can be really dumb? Somehow, Nicki interpreted my seeking to go to the prayer meeting as not wanting to be with her after this incredibly frightening event. Men and women are different, and that is one of the primary differences. Women see their husband's leaving during a traumatic situation as "He doesn't care." Knowing that, we need to do the wise thing—stick around.

Remember, there is no one who is more important to you than the one going through cancer treatment. Don't do anything that would give her reason to think that you would rather be somewhere else.

Chapter 23

Two of my nieces just had babies, and a third is due in three months. Babies are such incredible blessings. The Bible states that they are a "gift from God." I think they are one of His most precious gifts. The amazing reality of babies is their total inability to do anything. They don't clean house, cook, make their beds, or take out the trash. They just look cute.

After a while, they begin to make noises and start crawling. Shortly thereafter, they say their first words and begin to stand. Sentences and steps follow, and then they begin to get around on their own. About twenty-four to thirty months after birth, an amazing event takes place. They take their words, put them into a coherent order, and begin to ask questions. "Why? How? When? Why? Who? Why? Why?" It seems the questions never stop. Some parents begin to go a little bit nuts as they try to deal with all of the hundreds of questions.

We usually solve this problem by sending our children to school. There they are told to be quiet. The questions don't stop, but their numbers are greatly reduced.

Then cancer strikes. In panic, we go to the doctor, receive a diagnosis, are told what treatment to endure, and hope things work out. The idea of asking a lot of questions almost seems taboo. After all, aren't they doctors? The father of the twelve tribes of Israel was Isaac's son, Jacob. During a difficult time in his life, an angel of the Lord visited him, and they wrestled. Jacob refused to let go until the angel blessed him. Because of his perseverance, God changed his name to Israel, which means "to wrestle with God." If it's all right to wrestle with God, why can't we wrestle with our medical team? We do this by asking questions.

Remember our first principle: stay in control. We do this by asking questions. You have hired your doctor to perform a service. Part of that service is to inform you of what is taking place and what the options are. They know more than you do and are entitled to respect. You are paying their salary and are also due respect.

For our first visit to Dr. Chong, someone suggested we take another person with us to take notes. It was a great idea. We were in shock and forgot most of what he said. We referred back to the notes taken by our friend on many occasions. In addition, you need to keep a notepad around so you can write any questions that come to you. This allows you to think through the questions and phrase them properly. Ask people who have gone through your situation what questions they wish they had asked. Read up on your illness. Questions will come to you. Bounce questions off of your family members and support team.

Remember also our second principle "Don't be afraid to ask questions." Ask your doctors questions, but don't abuse their time and don't insult their intelligence by asking silly questions. The purpose of the questions is to give you answers, but also to give you peace of mind about those to whom you are entrusting your life.

We asked our oncologist why she didn't order a PET scan. She replied, "Because you are a low-risk patient." The question led to an answer that gave us hope and peace. Ask those questions.

Chapter 24

Several years ago, I decided to read through the entire Bible and find every verse that dealt with the subjects of encouragement, discouragement, courage, and support. Out of my study came a fifteen-message sermon series on the topic of encouragement. In preparing those messages, I read more than a dozen books on why people get discouraged and how to encourage them.

One of the most interesting aspects of that study was discovering what I consider to be the most unusual college facility in the United States. It is the University of Miami Institute for Touch. The University of Miami is very well known for its football and baseball programs, but this center may be the most significant part of the university.

The institute came about in an attempt to study premature babies. Their medical research proved invaluable in so many other areas of life. Babies that were held by their parents had a nearly 50 percent higher rate of recovery and left the hospital far sooner than babies that were left in isolation. This was later confirmed by orphanages in war-torn countries.

It also works with those recovering from cancer.

Every cancer is different, and every patient is different. However, breast cancer is especially traumatic for women. Our culture has over-saturated the media with sexual material and communicated to women that the only way to please a man is to be very well endowed. A recent survey revealed that one of the most popular gifts for upper-class female high school graduates is breast implants. That is disturbing. It is no wonder that women feel "less than a woman" if they lose a breast (or a portion of one).

This is where touching fits in. A loving husband will touch his wife. It doesn't have to have sexual overtones; in fact, it is better if it doesn't. Hold her hand. Hug her when she walks by. Put your hand on her shoulder. In a gentle, tender way, touch her. It is amazing, the response.

The University of Miami Institute is not the first group to discover this principle. One of the great stories in the Bible explained this principle. The most feared disease in the first century was leprosy. It was a death penalty and could be transferred in some cases by touch. We are told that ten lepers came to Jesus asking to be healed. He could have yelled at them from a distance to be healed. He didn't. Rather, he walked up to them and he laid hands on all ten.

He touched them. Find someone who is hurting and touch that person.

Chapter 25

Nicki had her first chemotherapy treatment today. After five hours, she felt pretty well. We had a bowl of soup, she took a nap, and she took her anti-nausea medication. Then it all hit. Her body ached, her head hurt, and she began to throw up. We even had a conversation on people who use marijuana to ease the pain. Her nausea lasted for nearly four days.

When you experience either the ravages of cancer or the reaction to its treatment, it is not difficult to understand why someone would contemplate illegal drugs, suicide, or other responses. There is another response.

Perseverance!

That is easier for me to say, since I am not the one who has to take the chemotherapy. I am the one having to deal with its consequences. I keep telling my wife, "You will get through this." That is not just wishful thinking.

The Wall Street Journal ran an article on treating cancer aggressively. They reported the success rates of treatments for the various types of cancer. The cure rate for women diagnosed with breast cancer is now up to 89 percent. That is nine out of ten. That is good news. It means that Nicki will probably get through this.

There is a great verse in the Bible. It states of Jesus that, *"for the joy set before Him, He endured the cross"* (Hebrews 12:2 NIV). Chemotherapy is not the end; it is the means to an end. We endure the treatment because of what it will gain us when it is all over: life with our loved ones. As you endure the pain, remember that there is joy at the end.

Chapter 26

Recently, my wife had two chairs re-upholstered for my office. When we went to pick up the chairs, we saw a store across the street that my wife had wanted to go through. There was a bookstore right next to it, so we were both happy.

She was able to pick up a couple of scarves but did not find any hats that she liked. We then began to talk about wigs. In all her years of dealing with the public, Nicki has only seen one wig that looked like the person's real hair, and that cost over a thousand dollars. We have all seen and joked about wigs and toupees that look like they were purchased at a garage sale. However, the one looking for a wig does not see this as a laughing matter. The person has lost his or her hair. It can be a traumatic experience.

Here is what we have learned. Everyone has an opinion. They like wigs, or they think wigs look funny. They think you should buy one, or they tell you not to waste your money. Their mothers wore wigs, or their mothers wouldn't be caught dead in wigs.

Remember what we said about getting too many opinions? This is one area in which that is certainly true. Only one person has to wear the wig or look for alternatives. That is you. We spend too much time asking, "What will people think"? In the scheme of what is really important, what others think should rank pretty low.

The important question is, "What do you think?" Then go for it. I believe that our highest allegiance should be God, but the old adage, "To thine own self be true" does apply in this case. You have to live with your decision, no one else. In matters of how you look, do what pleases you. Your real friends will understand, and the others don't count.

Chapter 27

Normandy, Gettysburg, the Alamo, Valley Forge. Our nation is filled with stories of great heroism and courage. There is another word that describes those events: *sacrifice*. The greatness of our nation has been its willingness to sacrifice for the well-being of others, even people we don't know.

Cancer brings out the best and worst in people. We are often physically exhausted, emotionally drained, and spiritually dry. We also can reach down and find resources we did not know we had.

Overcoming cancer is about sacrifice. I had to sacrifice my time. I keep a busy schedule. There are always people to meet with, things to do, books to read, and articles to write. Sitting in a doctor's office for three hours is not my idea of using my time wisely. However, Nicki needed me there. I don't like just sitting, but I do like my wife. Therefore, I sacrifice.

There is another person who needs to sacrifice as well: the one with cancer. One might think that having cancer is a big enough sacrifice. It is obviously the greatest hardship imaginable. However, there are other sacrifices that need to be made. Life goes on, even for the family battling cancer. Bills need to be paid, school assignments need to be finished, and work schedules need to be kept. Unless you are independently wealthy, income needs to be generated. This means family will not always be at your beck and call. This is where support groups can be very helpful. Friends, neighbors, and people you know are usually willing to give of their time in short blocks. If you need to be in bed, coordinate a list of people who can each come by for two-hour periods. Many churches have ministries such as this for their members.

We have learned the truth of "banking kindness." Over the years, we have invested our lives ministering to people with no thought of being paid back. During this difficult period of time, all those investments have matured and are returning to bless us.

Here are two things to think about. First, don't wait until you need help to plug in to people. Begin now to develop a support team. It will bless them and encourage you. Second, talk through the areas of sacrifice each family member needs to make. Look for creative ways to do things. For instance, you could fold clothes or wash dishes while watching your favorite show. Be creative.

Just a reminder: sacrifice is at the heart of love.

Chapter 28

Nicki and I have been married for twenty-seven years. In that time, I have gotten angry twice. I have many weaknesses, but losing my emotional balance is not one of them. That number increased to three last week. I lost it. I mean, I really lost it. Nicki had gotten over the hard part of her first chemotherapy treatment, but she was feeling very tired. She made several comments, I got really ticked off, and I did some things that I regretted.

I could pretend it didn't happen, I could blame her, or I could apologize. That is what I did. We then talked and got several important issues out in the open. When all was said and done, she resented the fact that I hadn't cried over the fact that she had developed cancer. In her mind, not crying equaled not caring. I started to cry. I hate to cry, but it came out.

Men and women are different. Unless this is totally understood, real conflicts will arise. If the one with cancer is female and she expects her husband to react like a woman, she is going to build up a lot of resentment. What to do with this problem?

First, everyone needs to understand and respond to the illness in their own way. We do not all react the same. If your loved ones ignore you, deal with that. Otherwise, let your family react as they feel most comfortable. Don't expect them to react as you would; they aren't you.

Second, you will say and do things you will regret. Deal with those regretful words and actions with love and humility. Don't hold grudges, and don't build up resentments. Say you are sorry and get on with building your life.

Third, give your family some room to make mistakes. You probably wish you didn't have cancer. They also wish you didn't have cancer. You may be in unfamiliar territory, but so are they. Books, articles, and news articles are available for those with cancer. Oftentimes, the family members are left out in the cold. They have a burden to carry and often don't know how to deal with it. To vent sometimes creates guilt because they think they are creating stress for the one battling cancer. Give them some room to respond.

Fourth, you need to talk. Have open and frank discussions with everyone in the inner circle. Let people express themselves. If they are fearful or angry or feel left out, they need to say that to someone.

Fifth, play fair. You know information about those close to you that can devastate them. Don't use it. In your frustration, keep your lips sealed. You will never regret it.

The Bible is a very wise book, especially regarding how to respond in this situation. James 1:19 *NASB* states, *"Be quick to hear, slow to speak, and slow to anger."* That is pretty good advice.

Chapter 29

Exercise is a good thing. I enjoy walking. It keeps my weight down and also helps in my fight with cholesterol. My wife, on the other hand, loves going to her water aerobics class. After being diagnosed with cancer, she wanted to keep up her water aerobics class, but because of chemotherapy her immune system was compromised. She was advised by her oncologist not to swim because of possible bacteria in the pool.

While my wife and I love spending time together, I really enjoy walking alone. With my busy schedule, this is one of the few times when I can just relax. I have no decisions to make and no one's problems to solve, and I don't have to talk. I also use this time to listen to audio recorded messages. I record talk radio broadcasts in the morning and listen to them on my walks. I also listen to sermons that relate to messages I'm preparing or classes I'm teaching.

Nicki needed to exercise, but she couldn't swim. I like to walk, but I would rather walk alone. What to do? We solved the problem this way: I get up a little earlier and go for my two-mile walk by myself. Then, if she is up to it, we will walk the half-mile down to a local coffee shop, or walk a mile at night around the block.

Exercise is good for everyone. It is especially good for those recovering from cancer. Nicki needs to walk to keep her strength up. Scientists have learned that exercise releases endorphins, which aid in the healing process and act as an energy boost for the brain. In other words, exercise is brain food.

The individual who is battling cancer needs to exercise. The one giving support needs to encourage the other to exercise. This is an area in which sacrifice is necessary. The support team needs to sacrifice their desires for rest or for an individual exercise program so they can minister to the one recovering from cancer. Don't have him or her run a marathon, but make sure he or she gets in some exercise, even if it is to the corner and back. The person's life depends on it. It is good for you, too.

Chapter 30

Two more floral arrangements arrived this afternoon. In the five weeks after Nicki's surgery, we received about thirty-five flower arrangements, beginning with "the big one." What was interesting concerning all of these flowers was the fact that very few of them came on the same day. They almost all came on different days.

Surgeries and flowers have gone together for a long time. It is customary to send flowers after someone has had an illness or a surgery. It is not unusual for someone to receive many arrangements after a difficult surgery. Usually, though, they arrive within a few days after the actual surgery. We were blessed by having them come for weeks. It was Jesus Himself who promised, "Give and it will be given unto you." That is a promise we have seen fulfilled on so many different levels.

We have spent our adult lives ministering to the needs of people. From those seeds planted over the years, we are reaping an incredible harvest of love and gratitude. While flowers can be given without much thought, most are sent with love, concern, and compassion. People send flowers because they care.

During Nicki's time in the hospital, she asked me if I thought anyone loved her. I laughed and said, "Of course people love you." I thought she said it in a joking way. She was very serious. All of the love she has been given in the weeks after her surgery has demonstrated to her that my words of affirmation were true. Those who love others are usually loved in return.

One of the great movies of all time is *It's a Wonderful Life*. George Bailey spent his entire adult life trying to leave Bedford Falls so that he could discover the world. He was never able to leave because people continued to need him to bail them out from one disaster after another. When his uncle Billy lost a large sum of money that was to be deposited in the bank, George thought he was going to be arrested. It was then that the word went out to the townspeople that George needed help, and he learned that as someone who had friends, "He was the richest man in town."

We have discovered what we always knew. We are rich because we have friends who love us.

Chapter 31

Every year, nearly $4 billion in gift certificates are not redeemed in the United States. That is one of the reasons businesses promote them—they receive the money without having to give out the product. It makes good business sense. The other side of gift certificates is that the vast majority are used. People go out to restaurants, shop at stores, and purchase items they normally would not use because someone gave them a gift certificate.

When I decided to give Nicki a mammogram, I went to the Nancy Reagan Breast Center in Simi Valley. They have an excellent reputation in our community and perform mammograms for a reasonable cost. Sitting down at the front desk, I asked the receptionist if they had gift certificates for mammograms. I was surprised to learn that they did not. During October, they offer mammograms at a reduced rate, but they have nothing in writing to use as a gift enticement for women to come in for the procedure.

I asked how much they charged for a mammogram, went to the Hallmark store, purchased a Valentine's card, wrote out a check for the right amount, and gave it to my wife. Somehow, a check doesn't have the power that a gift certificate does. My wife thought I was giving her money to go shopping. My gift was much more valuable than clothes.

I went about seeking to develop some sort of gift certificate for hospitals and health centers to use as an encouragement for men to give mammograms to the women in their life. I think I came up with a winner: "mom-ograms."

It is obviously a take-off on the term *mammogram,* but it also has an emotional tug to it. How many men and women have lost a mother to cancer because it wasn't diagnosed early enough? How many husbands have children and would like their kids' mom to stick around for a long time? How many grandparents dread the idea of their grandchildren losing their mom to cancer? There are few people in our nation who are not touched by "Mom" and would give anything if they could get her back.

Do the next thing! Buy her a "mom-ogram." It just might save her life.

Chapter 32

⇨ ⇨ ⇨

You are what you eat. At least, that is how the saying goes. What we eat is important. This is especially true as you do battle with a serious disease. The problem comes down to defining what a healthy diet looks like. We have some new friends who have been very beneficial in our healing regimen. They order organic vegetables from Carmel, California, and have them shipped to them. Some might see that as extreme. Others would agree wholeheartedly with their decision.

The eating habits of the American family have changed drastically over the past several decades. We eat out more, exercise less, and eat more junk food than ever before. Growth hormones and other food additives have created unique problems for families seeking to eat healthily. There are several steps we took that did not require we go out and become extremists.

We talked with people who were doing it already. Even talking to those with extreme views can be helpful in seeking to balance everything out. They will give you their extreme views, which can be run through your lifestyle to come out with a plan that works for you. Most people involved in this lifestyle are not extreme. They are simply seeking to eat food that doesn't endanger the health of their family.

Friends gave us a juicer. This allowed us to get all of the vitamins and nutrients from the fruits and vegetables. We treated this as a supplement to our regular meals, and not as the normal meal.

We began shopping at markets that catered to the healthy eater. "Health food stores" have their place but are often very expensive, limited in their selection, and not as tasty. Stores such as Trader Joe's and Whole Foods Markets sell natural food without the "health food store" limits.

We began a garden. My wife loves working in the soil. We grew tomatoes, squash, herbs, and peppers. The more land you have, the bigger the garden you can create. There is a commitment necessary in this. You have to weed, water, and cultivate your plants.

We began eating out less frequently and when we did, at better places. If we went out for fast food, we tried to find one with a salad bar instead of fries and ordered fruit instead of fried potatoes. We would purchase deli sandwiches and go to the park, and we often split meals. We asked for nutritional charts. It is amazing how many items are labeled as "healthy" but have hidden fat and calories. Do your homework, and then you can choose wisely.

Most bookstores have entire sections on healthy eating cookbooks. Some Authors have placed emphasis on butter, creams, and exotic dishes. However, many are known for low-fat, good-tasting recipes. It is easy to choose one that is right for you and your family.

Soups and salads have become a staple of our diet. We love soup. It takes a little effort to make, but it is usually inexpensive, tastes good, and is good for us. We make a giant pot and put it in freezer containers. It is then available when we want a quick, healthy meal.

When you make healthy meals, you need to watch out for hidden enemies. This will usually show up in your soup stocks and additions. Many are high in salt and fats. Most stores now carry chicken, beef, and vegetable stocks that are fat-free, but still good-tasting. Use chicken that is skinless and lean ham or Canadian bacon with no nitrates instead of bacon. If you want beef in your soup, pre-cook it and skim off the fat.

We all have to eat. God created food to be enjoyed and to be beneficial to our use. Become informed on what is beneficial and what isn't.

Remember our rule: you need to stay in control. That includes what you eat. It takes time, but your health is worth it.

Chapter 33

One of the most popular attractions at the circus is the juggler. Some of them juggle bowling pins, some use flaming sticks, and one even uses chainsaws. One of the funniest jugglers places a dinner plate on a tall pole and spins it so fast that it will balance on its own. He then places another plate on a pole and spins that one so that it balances. He does this repeatedly so that he may have ten to twelve plates spinning at one time. Eventually, the first plate begins to wobble, and he has to run back and spin it or it will fall down. The crowd begins to laugh hysterically, as he now has to run back and forth between poles to keep them spinning so they will not crash.

For many people, that is a normal day. We get up in the morning and find which plate is just about ready to crash and give it a good spin. Then we go to the next pole. Then someone calls on the phone and asks if we can add another pole to the mix. By the end of the day, we are exhausted from trying to keep the plates from crashing down. There is no doubt that the average family has too many plates spinning, with no hope of relief in the immediate forecast. This creates tension, which creates anxiety, which produces stress, which produces negative enzymes in our blood, which open the door to all sorts of illnesses and problems. There are some solutions.

The best way to overcome stress is to rest. God knew what He was doing when He commanded His people to work for six days and rest on the seventh day. This command has two distinct instructions. The first is to work. Too much leisure is not good for us. The second instruction is to rest. Too much work is not good for us either. The Jewish Sabbath had a positive result in the life of those who observed that practice. Jews today who observe the Sabbath are better off physically. While Christians are not bound by the Sabbath laws, God still wants His people to take time and rest.

The ability to say no is a wonderful tool. Remember that our first cardinal rule of health is to stay in control. When you say no to someone, you are staying in control. There needs to be a balance in this. If all you do is say no to people so you can do whatever your little heart desires, you are simply being selfish. You do need to interact with others, and be a part of their lives. This means you need to pitch in and say yes to certain activities and events.

However, that does not mean you say yes to everything. You need to know your limits, and you need to be motivated by love and responsibility and not by guilt.

You need to learn to delegate. If you are overwhelmed, find someone who has less on their plate and teach them to do your job. Nicki had several responsibilities at our church. We knew she was overextended, but it was hard to give up those responsibilities. When her biopsy came back positive, it was not such a difficult task to delegate. Don't wait too long. Maybe some things won't get done, but that is all right. The sun will still come up tomorrow.

Let yourself fail once in a while. The key to learning how to juggle is to understand that you will drop a plate now and then. A person who can't drop a plate will never learn to juggle. Everything doesn't have to be done perfectly. Lighten up just a little and you will be amazed at how life does go on, even if the bed isn't made, the dishes aren't washed, and the floor isn't mopped. Get those around you to help. They need to learn responsibility too. However, remember that you are loved because you are you, not because you are perfect.

Chapter 34

"Is there anything I can do to help?" In our journey toward wellness, we have probably heard that question a hundred times. In most instances, we answer by saying, "Pray for us." We believe in the power of prayer and want thousands on our prayer team. However, there are people who feel the need to lend a physical hand.

If you have invested in the life of others for any length of time, their desire will be to pay you back. You have blessed them, and they feel it is now their turn to bless you. Why do we seem to be embarrassed to let people help us? The Bible tells us, *"God is opposed to the proud but gives grace to the humble"* (James 4:6 NASB). Pride often prevents us from allowing people to minister to us. We don't let people come over to clean our house because they will see how dirty it is. We don't want them to cook for us because we don't want handouts. The truth is that God allows us to have needs so that others will have an opportunity to demonstrate their love to us. Pride will not only prevent people from demonstrating love, but it will also force God Himself to come in and deal with us.

One of the means by which God blesses us is by giving us friends who care enough to help. When we refuse to let them follow up on this God-created desire, we wound their spirits. Knowing this in advance, preplan your response. If they can't cook, don't ask them to bring in a meal. If they aren't financially ahead, don't ask them to pay a bill. Think through some of the things you do need and respond accordingly. Here are some suggestions you can give people who want to help you.

Take your children to a park or a movie. You need the rest, and your kids need to have fun.

Fix a meal. This would be for dinner that evening. They would bring it in hot and provide the entire meal.

Fix a meal for later. Bring in a medley of fruit, a meatloaf for the freezer, soup, casserole, or barbecued chicken for the refrigerator are all suggestions. These can be brought in and saved for meals when you feel better.

Mow the lawn, trim the flowers, or weed.

Laundry. They can wash and dry, with you putting the clothes away.

Wash windows.

Harvest the garden.

Clean out the garage.

Read you a book.

Clean house.

Babysit.

Be creative, know the people who are asking, and give them the assignment for which they are equipped. You will be encouraged, and your friends will be blessed because they had an opportunity to give back to you for all you have done for them.

Chapter 35

Nicki's hair began to fall out today. It has been two months since her surgery and two weeks since her first chemotherapy treatment. We knew it was coming, but tomorrow would have been a better day.

Nicki has been looking for hats, found some nice scarves, and was emotionally ready for this day. But tomorrow would have been better.

There is a great Scripture for situations like this. It begins the Christmas story, and it simply states, "And it came to pass . . ." There are no magic cures for losing your hair, dealing with the death of a loved one, facing a tragedy, or experiencing the betrayal of a friend. There is only one thing you can do as you face your "valley of the shadow of death."

You have to walk through it!

You can't ignore it, make light of it, overemphasize it, or pray it away. You must go through it. Jesus faced His Gethsemane. Millions have faced tragedies throughout the centuries. Nicki had to face losing her hair. You will need to face your valley.

Walk through it.

There is a wonderful promise in the Bible for such a time as this. The name God gives Himself is Jehovah. Periodically, a situation arose among the Jews that created a special need in their midst. God would often come to them and remind them of who He was. He would do this by adding an adjective to His name. It was sort of a nickname. Once, He told Gideon that He was Jehovah-Shalom, "the God of peace." That is a wonderful promise. On another occasion, He gave Himself the name Jehovah-Shammah. It simply means "The God who is always there."

God reminds us of His presence in so many ways. Often, he gives us friends. They cannot take your burden away. They cannot carry your burden. However, they can carry you.

Let them!

Chapter 36

Cancer strikes one individual, but it affects the entire family. This is true of any life-threatening illness. Everyone else's schedule has to change to accommodate the one with the disease. Our youngest daughter graduated from college the week before Nicki received the results of her biopsy. Once we knew the results, she decided to postpone returning to college to gain her teaching credential for one semester. Our other daughter adjusted her work schedule to be available for various situations. Both girls did this on their own because they wanted to.

However, the vast majority of attention goes to the individual going through the treatment. That is appropriate and expected. This sometimes leaves the rest of the family, especially the children, out in the dark.

We have a program in our church that we call "secret prayer partners." Some groups have "secret sisters" or other such names. Each year, the women of our church each pull out the name of another lady and promise to pray for her every day. It is not required, but many ladies also give birthday, anniversary, and holiday gifts.

The Sunday after Nicki made the announcement that she had cancer, a little box was placed on the back table with my oldest daughter's name attached. The card simply stated that her prayer partner was praying for her. Inside the box was a beautiful, little, pink ceramic ribbon. The pink ribbon is the symbol of the fight against breast cancer. It was her prayer partner's way of telling Erin that she was not alone.

Don't forget to support the kids. They are hurting too.

Chapter 37

Nicki had her head shaved today. It was a pre-emptive action to her hair falling out, but it brought tears. It is one of the differences between men and women. It is cool for men to shave their heads if it looks like they might be going bald. There are few women's magazines that have advocated the bald look as the next sexy image.

Because we live in an image-driven culture, how women look is important to how they feel. A woman's hair is a big part to how she looks; therefore, a woman's hair is important to her image.

Can this issue be overcome?

I have done an extensive study on ego and self-image. Our culture has made self-image the end-all of any discussion. Public schools have turned entire curriculum topics into attempts to improve the self-image of their students. Schools have canceled sports programs because they think that students on the losing team will have a poor self-image. Teachers have given students high grades for poor work because they don't want to harm their self-image. Students are smart enough to figure out what is taking place. Students gain a positive self-image when they believe they have done their best and are rewarded accordingly.

I do not believe a positive self-image is created by teaching students they have succeeded when they know that they haven't. A good self-image is based on something far more important. Self-image is based largely on what an individual perceives to be how the most important person in the individual's life sees him or her. If the most important person in my life thinks I'm a loser, I will probably have a poor self-image. If the person I care the most about thinks I'm wonderful, my self-image will rise.

The most important person in Nicki's life does not love her because she has beautiful hair. He loves her because she is worth loving. That is why He died on a cross outside the city of Jerusalem and came out of the tomb three days later. He wanted her to know that she was worth dying for.

Her husband thinks she is beautiful too!

P.S. God loves you too!

Chapter 38

"How do you feel?" We have all asked that question hundreds of times. Usually we don't expect a response. It is designed as a rhetorical question. We ask the question as a gracious gesture, but we don't really expect others to tell us how they really feel. They are supposed to say, "I feel good, how about yourself?" We then answer, "I feel good, thank you." Then we are free to go about our business.

When you are facing cancer, that question is not easy to handle. The reason for this is the people who ask the question. Most of them really do want to know how you feel. They are not asking a rhetorical question. This can create some tension because there are not very many times when you actually do feel fine. One week, you have chemotherapy; the next week, you learn that your white cell count is down; and the third week, you begin to think about your chemo treatment the next week. You get tired of telling people that you don't feel all that well.

The best way to deal with this question is be up front. There is no reason to be upset or frustrated with the question. It is acceptable to say, "I usually feel pretty tired, but thanks for your concern." It certainly isn't inappropriate to ask for their prayers. If you have a good support team, acknowledge their positive influence in your life. To say, "I was really depressed yesterday, but some dear friends came by with flowers or a meal, and I am doing much better now" lets the questioner know your situation and also gives that person an opportunity to become a part of your support team. That is a good thing.

You need to remember one of the cardinal rules of cancer. We don't ask why; we ask, "What now?" Pre-plan some answers to various questions. If the question is inappropriate, don't be afraid to say, "I'd rather not talk about that now." There are some very insensitive people in your life; don't let them control you. Simply move on. A gracious answer is a powerful reply to those who are insensitive.

Chapter 39

Art Linkletter was a broadcasting pioneer who created, "Kids say the darndest things." He spent a lifetime interviewing children, and some of their comments were absolutely hilarious. Were he to coin that phrase today, it might come out, "Adults can say the most inappropriate things." We had someone come up right after we announced that Nicki had been diagnosed with cancer and say to us, "You take your chemotherapy, and half die and half live." The odds of success are actually much better than fifty-fifty, but we didn't argue. Another person wrote us a letter to inform us that all of his close relatives had died of cancer.

When these insensitive comments are made, you have a choice to make. You can become angry with their insensitivity, or you can ignore the statement and get on with your healing. Life is too short to hold grudges. Anger and bitterness can have a negative impact on your healing process. Don't let that happen.

You cannot stop people from saying dumb things, but you can control how you respond. Be gracious. Be forgiving. When you get alone, laugh and be grateful as to your fortune in not waking up to that attitude every morning. Have a support group that overcomes those stupid statements with positive, life-affirming words. It is a much better response.

Chapter 40

Millicent Kondracke passed away July 22, 2004. Known as Millie by those close to her, she was the wife of Mort Kondracke, Fox News commentator and editor of *Roll Call* magazine. After a seventeen-year battle with Parkinson's disease, Millie said a final good-bye and entered into eternity.

By all accounts, the Kondrackes had a great marriage. It was not always that way. Mort drank too much and spent too much time at work. He wanted to work his way up the newsroom ladder. Parkinson's changed that. Through their seventeen-year battle, they truly bonded. Along with actor Michael J. Fox, the Kondrackes led the fight to see more federal money used on Parkinson's research. Toward the end of the battle, Mort wrote a best-selling book entitled *Saving Millie*. In an interview concerning the book, Mort shared his opinion that the book was misnamed. He stated that the title should have been *Saving Mort*. While Millie was the one with the disease, Mort came to realize how Parkinson's had come to redeem his life when he was on the way to alcoholism and a well-paying but meaningless career. Millie's illness forced Mort to reevaluate his life and make some career decisions. Those decisions meant that he would never be the editor of the *Washington Post*. It also meant that he would have a life of significance and the love of a great woman.

Whether it is Parkinson's, leukemia, cancer, or a tragic accident, everything changes. The issue facing us is do we allow this hurdle to be a positive change or a negative one? Remember cardinal rule #3: "Don't ask why—ask, 'What now?'" That rule allows us to move on from the terrible ordeal and on to a life of significance. The Kondrackes asked, "What now?" and decided to fight the illness, refuse to give in to their weaknesses, and draw close to each other. Nicki and I made that same decision. It makes all the difference.

Chapter 41

We will all die. For most of us, it will be many years from now. Each of us, though, will be the focal point of a funeral service. We don't like to discuss death, but it is a reality of life. We might as well deal with it in an honest and open way.

I raise this subject because it is one of the most important issues in facing a potentially terminal illness. The first time you hear those words, "You have cancer" (leukemia, Parkinson's, etc.), your first thought is *What can I do so that she/he doesn't die?* The truth is there is nothing you can do to assure them that the person will not die. Death is inevitable. It is one of the few certainties of life.

The right question to ask is, "What do I need to do so that she/he can live a little longer?" The Kondrackes made several significant decisions that added years to Millie's life. It didn't prevent her death, but it added years to their marriage and made their relationship more significant.

Some relationships crumble under the weight of the stress. That is even more tragic than the illness. This is why the vows at most weddings talk about staying true "in sickness and in health, until death do us part." This is where life is lived. It is where love is produced. It is where significance is developed.

As Moses was preparing the children of Israel to enter the promised land, he stood before them and gave them a final decision. He stated, *"I call heaven and earth to witness against you today, that I have set before you life and death, the blessing and the curse. So choose life in order that you may live…"* (Deuteronomy 30:19 NASB).

A long life and healthy life are not guaranteed by God. However, those who choose to look illness and death in the face and say, "We will fight this, and we will draw closer to each other in the process" will find something far more valuable than a long life. They will find a blessed life.

Chapter 42

It is called friendly fire, and it is one of the most difficult aspects of warfare. Friendly fire occurs when an army accidentally kills its own soldiers. It usually happens when bombs are dropped off-target and land on your own troops. The Civil War changed dramatically when the Confederate army's best general, Thomas "Stonewall" Jackson, was accidentally shot by his own troops.

Any battle with a serious illness has to be considered a war. It is a life-and-death struggle with disease, viruses, and bacteria. Our weapons are not guns and bombs, but doctors, medicine, and friends. Every war has the danger of friendly fire taking place. When battling illnesses, it is important that this danger be dealt with.

Friendly fire can be overcome if you put into practice four principles. They are steps that work not only with this problem, but with any difficulty.

First, expect friendly fire to arise. Our emotions get the best of us, our bodies react negatively to medication, and we become exhausted with helping the one who is sick. Something has to give, and often it is our words. Expect it and you will be less likely to fall into this pit.

Second, take time to talk with those in your sphere of influence. If the one who is fighting the illness feels he or she is being neglected, the person needs to be able to share that. If the one giving care is feeling unappreciated and manipulated, he or she needs to be able to say that. Hurt feelings left unresolved often result in bitterness, which can lead to anger and even hatred. Talk through what you're feeling on both sides and communicate your love and frustrations. If one party refuses to talk or denies the feelings of the other, you need a third party to intervene. If the other person refuses, get ready for major problems down the road, because they will come. Serious illnesses are a difficult hurdle to overcome, but they do not give someone the right to be cruel.

Third, practice the Golden Rule. It was Jesus who said, "Do unto others as you would have them do unto you." Don't let hatred and bitterness stew. Overcome them with love and forgiveness. The Bible states, *"Love covers a multitude of sins"* (1 Peter 4:8 NASB). It is amazing what takes place when an angry individual is responded to in love and forgiveness. The hostility often falls away, and true communication can then take place.

Fourth, remember that you are in this together. You have a common bond and a common opponent. You are not enemies; you are partners. You want to be together after your trip through the valley, so hold your tongue when you want to lash out. You will not regret doing so.

Chapter 43

Experts tell us that we only know about 10 percent of all the information that will be available to us in 2025. What that tells us is that the "experts" don't know everything. This certainly is true in the medical field. Look at all of the miracle drugs and amazing surgeries that are now commonplace but were unavailable twenty years ago.

Nicki's first two chemotherapy sessions were totally different. After going through her first therapy session, we arrived home, put her in a relaxing chair, and proceeded to help her throw up for the next four days. Her anti-nausea medication was changed three times, and her stomach finally settled down. For her second treatment, they changed her anti-nausea medication completely. She did not throw up once, but she felt really drugged out for four days.

After she began to feel stronger, we talked about the differences in her treatments. She didn't like feeling so drugged up, but she forgot how sick she had felt following her first treatment. It was a reminder that our medical team doesn't have all the answers. They have spent years seeking as much information as possible. They know more than just about everyone else. They are experts in their field. However, we need to remember that much of the healing process is by trial and error.

As humans, we deal with illnesses differently. Some are affected by surgery more severely than others. We each respond to medication differently. This is why it is important to live by cardinal rule #1 and stay in control. The doctors and nurses know medications, illnesses, and medical theories. You know yourself. If a process isn't working, speak up. If you think something is going wrong, ask. Don't be disrespectful, but don't be intimidated either. The questions we asked were all answered and all proved our medical team to be accurate and on top of the situation. Most medical personnel are more than competent. Trust them in what they are saying and doing. However, they are not immune to mistakes and missed diagnoses. You are the one who has to live with the consequences of whatever transpires. Stay on top of the situation. As President Reagan used to say, "Trust, but verify." It is not a sin to question.

Chapter 44

What do you do with all of your free time? In going through the healing process, you have a lot of free time. Taking medication, resting, and doctor's visits are a normal part of the trip to wellness. What do you do while waiting? I read a lot. I read several papers every day, several weekly periodicals, a couple of monthly magazines, and dozens of books over the course of the year.

This book began as a means of dealing with my free time and working through the grief process. We received word last evening that a very dear friend had lost her battle with cancer. The family had known for several months that she would not survive and had begun the process of grieving. They will survive. That grief is different from what occurs when cancer is discovered but healing is expected. That is our situation.

I began to write as a means of trying to understand and explain what was going on in our journey through the valley. It has allowed me to remember how God has worked, whom to remember to thank, and what we have to be grateful for.

Everyone needs to find an outlet. Some may knit blankets for their grandchildren. Others will paint. A few will write. Take advantage of this unique opportunity to do something for yourself. In the process, you will leave a priceless treasure for those who follow in your footsteps.

Chapter 45

"Give and it will be given to you" (Luke 6:38 NASB) Those words of Jesus have never been truer than through our journey to wellness. Those who spend their lives ministering to others all face the same question at some point in their lives. It is the question "Is it worth it?" Obedience to God is always worth it, but we usually think of our rewards as coming in heaven.

There comes a time when all of us have to look at our lives to see if giving is really blessed by God in this life. When Nicki began her chemotherapy treatment, some friends of ours came by the house to let us know that a fundraiser had been set up for Nicki's medical expenses at one of the local pizza parlors. I mentioned this in a previous chapter.

The event is now behind us, and to say we were stunned would be an understatement. People had to order their pizzas and hand a bulletin to the cashier with Nicki's name on it for us to receive credit. Over a period of four hours, people came in at a rate of one per minute to order pizza. The money raised was beneficial, but the fellowship and encouragement were incredible. Nearly fifteen churches participated in the event, and people who had not seen each other for years rekindled old friendships.

This is the blessing of giving. When you give, it comes back to you. However, it doesn't just come back in dollars and cents. It comes back in the sacrifices of those to whom you have given, and it is then extended to others who are blessed by the fallout.

If you have not done so, learn to give. It will not only benefit you when you get to heaven, but will also bless you during your most difficult situations in life, as people who have been blessed by you will give back.

It is worth it!

Chapter 46

For some strange reason, I am having a hard time getting into my clothes. I think my daughters are washing my clothes in really hot water and shrinking everything.

Okay, maybe I have gained some weight. Nicki and I both became concerned about our weight about a year ago. My cholesterol went above the acceptable level. We began attending meetings for one of the nation's best weight loss organizations. Over the course of several months, we both lost twenty-five pounds.

When Nicki was diagnosed, we stopped attending meetings. Our priorities changed, and our schedules were upended. That is to say, we both gained back many of those pounds we had lost.

In dealing with cancer, or any other serious illness, it is easy to let things slide. Weight loss and weight gain are not high up the list of priorities. You have to eat what you can keep down and when you can work it in.

However, there is another side to that issue. Our weight is important in our healing process. Significant weight gain probably indicates that you are eating too much fat and starch and not enough fruits and vegetables. This was so in our case. Halfway through our treatment schedule, we recommitted ourselves to eat right and not let ourselves go. In our journey to wellness, losing weight was down the priority list, but eating healthy was a very high priority. When we eat healthy, we tend to lose weight. Keep your main things the main thing. Eat well. It will have positive consequences in many areas of your life.

Chapter 47

Cancer can be very depressing. Even those who survive, which is a majority today, find it difficult to be upbeat. After all, how easy is it to be excited about throwing up, blood draws, feeling tired, losing your hair, and high medical bills? There is not much to rejoice at in all of that. Nicki found a key to survive this journey through the valley to wellness.

Her doctor visits were scheduled every Wednesday. The first chemotherapy treatment made her very sick. For three days, she could keep no food down. If her bladder was full, her throwing up created other embarrassing situations. The fourth day saw relief with eating, and her strength began to return after the fifth day. On Wednesday, she had a doctor's visit to check her blood count. She was given a shot to increase her white cells, and she felt much better that week. On the next Wednesday, her blood count was normal, and she had a good week.

Then came chemotherapy treatment number two. Our oncologist changed Nicki's treatment, and she did not throw up. However, she felt very drugged and spent five days feeling very nauseated. On Wednesday, she went in for her blood work, and her white count was good. She also felt a little stronger. The third week was as normal as could be expected.

As we progressed through each treatment, we saw a pattern developing. The first week would be a bad week. During the second week, she was weak but could function. The third week would be back to normal.

Here is where the individual's attitude affects how he or she feels. As Nicki left the doctor's office after the second week of blood work, she realized the next Wednesday would be her chemotherapy session. She could look forward to her treatment, or she could enjoy a good week. When people asked her when her next treatment was planned, she would tell them but then put it out of her mind. This is living one day at a time, and it is critical to the emotional survival of those working through cancer.

What we focus our attention on will affect our well-being. If you focus on the pain that is to come, you will have six months of pain. If you allow yourself to focus on the good days, you will have bad days and good days.

Remember cardinal rule #10: "Get through the bad days and enjoy the good days." The bad days will come! However, they will also pass. Don't anticipate the bad days. They will come whether you want them to or not. Live today! That is the only time you actually have. Anticipate the good days and enjoy them with those you love. Endure the bad days, knowing they will pass. It will make the journey much more enjoyable.

Chapter 48

The worst fire in the history of the upper midwest occurred on October 8, 1871. Nearly fifteen hundred people died as hotels, schools, churches, and homes burned to the ground. The entire city was nearly destroyed. I doubt that 1 percent of our nation's population could name the city in which that fire took place because a hundred miles to the south, Mrs. O'Leary's cow had kicked over a lantern, beginning a small fire in Chicago.

While only two hundred and fifty people died in the Chicago fire, because it was a hub for communication and transportation, its story was heard around the nation. It was not until a week later that word was received that Peshtigo, Wisconsin, had burned to the ground. Because fire destroyed all of the telegraph lines, communication with the outside world was impossible. By the time help arrived, many of the survivors of the fire had died of starvation.

The old adage that the squeaky wheel gets the grease is true, often to the detriment of the individual. When you are dealing with a serious illness, you cannot afford to make decisions based on a squeaky wheel. You will receive all sorts of recommendations for treatments. Friends will tell you of elixirs and supplements that will work wonders. Many of them do. However, only you have the information that deals with your total program. This is one of the reasons we suggested at the beginning that you limit the number of sources you have for input. Check out the "magic elixirs." Examine the "miracle pills." You should research information on the medical advances taking place in your field of illness. However, do it in the privacy of your own secluded world. Let the people know how much you appreciate their concern. Thank those who pray for you and who give you books, magazines, and articles to read. However, do not sit down for any sales presentations. Your life and your health are too important for you to make a decision based on the pressure of a loved one or a slick promoter.

Remember cardinal rule #1: "Stay in control." Do what you do based on what you are convinced is in your best interest, not based on pressure from others or a desire not to displease a loved one. The stakes are too high to make decisions based on any other reason than "this is what works best for me." Then stick to it.

Chapter 49

Oops! We missed our chemotherapy treatment. Actually, we were forty-five minutes late, but because it was an afternoon appointment, we did not have enough time for all that was needed to be done. Our appointment was rescheduled for the next morning.

We were perplexed about what happened. Nicki is very meticulous in all that she does, which is why she is a good interior designer. She had taken the card from the doctor's office and wrote into her calendar book a 2:45 p.m. appointment. The doctor's office had her scheduled for 2:00 p.m. Since the therapy takes about three hours, we had to reschedule.

It makes sense that the appointment would be at 2:00 p.m. It is also a fact that Nicki is usually pretty accurate. The issue isn't who was right or what the right time was. The issue is that it is always a good policy to confirm your appointment. Many doctor's offices call the day before to remind patients of their appointments. Our oncologist does not do that. Therefore, it is our responsibility to be accurate.

I have a friend who defines punctuality as "treating other people's time as more important than your own." Most people resent sitting in a doctor's waiting room for a long time. We think, "If they can't take me until 4:00, why do they have me come in at 3:30?" It is a fair question and one that will not be answered here. It is one of the reasons I always take a book to a doctor's appointment. We have no control over what takes place in the doctor's office. We can control what takes place in our world. Confirm your appointments, be on time, don't gripe, and bring a book. It will help you make the best use of your time.

Chapter 50

They are called unintended consequences and can have either positive or negative reactions. As an illustration, let's say that you are on your way to a job interview and just before you arrive, the car in front of you swerves off of the road because of a flat tire. Do you pull over and see if they need help? Do you pass them by and go to your interview? Would it help you to decide if you knew that the driver was the wife of the president of the company for which you were interviewing?

Unintended consequences are the benefits or problems that occur because of your actions that were not anticipated. You did not anticipate being hired for this new job because you helped someone change a flat. You didn't expect to have your interview cancelled because you failed to help someone change a flat. Those are the unintended consequences, and we see them in our lives all the time.

When our friends scheduled the pizza fundraiser, we felt awkward and a little weird, but because they loved us, we accepted their generosity. The evening was a tremendous success as literally hundreds of people ordered pizzas, shared fellowship, and expressed their love to us.

Something else took place. Many people were both unable to participate in the fundraiser and unavailable to attend that evening. So they mailed in checks. In addition, several churches in our community also gave generous donations to our medical fund. When everything was added up, the fundraiser was a great success. The amount raised, though, was matched by the checks mailed in by friends and also by the amount sent in by other congregations. In other words, the amount raised at the actual fundraiser was only a third of the total amount raised. Our friends intended to raise money by selling pizzas, but the unintended consequence was that money came in by other means, which tripled the total amount raised.

If you have a need and someone says he or she wants to help you, let them. Even if little money is raised at the actual event, you can never know what the unintended consequences will be. Maybe some money will be raised. Maybe some friends will be encouraged. Maybe you will unintentionally help someone who will find you a job.

Chapter 51

We had been going to our oncology appointments for about ten weeks before I saw it. On the wall was posted an information sheet announcing that the Mars Candy Company had created a new line of pink and white M&M candies. A certain amount of each purchase went to fund cancer research. Fundraisers are major events these days. MDA raises nearly a million dollars every Labor Day for Muscular Dystrophy. The US Post Office offers a breast cancer awareness postage stamp. All of us have purchased Girl Scout cookies because "It is a good cause."

Several years ago, both of our daughters came home from school and announced that they were going to participate in the Southern California Avon Breast Cancer Three-Day Walk. Between the two of them, they raised more than $2,500. Their participation in that fundraiser changed their lives. The testimonies of those who had survived cancer blessed their hearts.

As the walk began, all of the participants gathered in the parking lot at the Earl Warren Fairgrounds in Santa Barbara, California. Suddenly, Gloria Gainer's "I Will Survive" was blasted over the speakers, and hundreds of cancer survivors, all wearing pink hats, led the procession through Santa Barbara on their way to Ventura. At the end of the three days, all of the cancer survivors received pink tee shirts.

After calling our parents to let them know that Nicki had been diagnosed with breast cancer, we told the girls. After tears and hugs, one of them stated to Nicki, "Just think; now you will be able to wear a pink hat." Rather than react with fear of their mom dying, their involvement in the Avon walk taught them that many women diagnosed with cancer survive.

They were not thinking, "My mom has cancer; she is going to die." They were thinking, "My mom has cancer; she will survive!" It is a good reason to encourage your children to participate in acts of charity. They often learn truths that are far more important than how to raise money.

Chapter 52

Under the best of circumstances chemotherapy is difficult. One person told my wife that each treatment was worse than the one before. Someone else said that the third and sixth treatments were the worst. Another person told us that her mother was a rock climber and the week after her final chemotherapy treatment, she climbed Mount Whitney.

Following Nicki's first treatment, she was violently ill. After the second treatment, she felt drugged out. The third treatment left her very depressed. This has led us to a pretty clear observation. Everyone responds differently. This is why they do a blood check each off week. In some cases, Nicki's white cell count was acceptable. On some occasions, it was borderline. A few times, it was low.

Listen to those who want to share their experiences. It is beneficial to them. However, it is important to understand that regardless of how they reacted to their chemotherapy, you will be different. You will not even react the same way to each one of your own treatments. Have no expectations other than the reality that you will get through it. You will have good days and you will have bad days, but you will survive chemotherapy.

That much you can count on.

Chapter 53

A man was walking through a cemetery looking at the writing on the tombstones. Most of them had the name of the deceased and the dates of his or her birth and death. Every once in a while, he wandered upon one that had something to say. One caught his attention. It read, "Here lies John Smith. Died: age twenty-five. Buried: age seventy-four." So many people go through life taking time to do that which is not all that important. If you are dealing with cancer, either yourself or a family member, why do you want to get well? If God gives you another twenty or thirty years, what do you plan on doing with it?

The average American spends eight months of his or her life opening junk mail. We spend two years returning phone calls, five years standing in lines, one year looking for lost items (probably more in my case), and six months waiting at stoplights. With those statistics in mind, what do you plan on doing with the extended time you are asking God to give you?

Just something to think about.

Chapter 54

God allows tragedies to happen to good people. I do not know why; I only know that to be true. The Old Testament is filled with bad things happening to godly people and then God making something good come out of that tragedy. The New Testament is a story of people seeking to do God's will and going through difficult times.

Your life is probably a testimony of blessings and tragedies. Where is God in all of this? The most famous chapter in the entire Bible is Psalm 23. It states,

> *"The Lord is my shepherd; I shall not want. He makes me lie down in green pastures; he leads me beside the still waters. He restores my soul; He leads me in the paths of righteousness for His name's sake. Yea, though I walk through the valley of the shadow of death, I will fear no evil; for You are with me; Your rod and Your staff, they comfort me. You prepare a table before me in the presence of my enemies; You anoint my head with oil; my cup runs over. Surely goodness and mercy shall follow me all the days of my life; and I will dwell in the house of the Lord forever."* (Psalms 23, NKJV)

That passage has comforted millions over the centuries. It is critical that you understand this passage. Nowhere in these words is an explanation for why the trial you are experiencing came to be. God does not explain why He does what He does. This passage gives us a far more important reality. God's desire is to comfort us in the midst of difficult situations.

That may be hard for some to comprehend. In the midst of a tragedy, we are angry at whomever or whatever caused it. Since God claims to be all-powerful, let's blame Him. It is here that a decision must be made. We can blame, or we can be comforted. There is time to seek blame where it is appropriate. However, if you are in the midst of the storm, seek comfort. It is available.

Chapter 55

Joseph was a common name in the Bible. The human father of Jesus had that name. So did the son of Jacob, who delivered his entire family line after being sold into slavery by his brothers.

There is another Joseph in early church history. We read: *"Now Joseph, a Levite of Cyprian birth, who was also called Barnabas by the apostles (which translated means 'son of encouragement'), and who owned a tract of land, sold it and brought the money and laid it at the apostles' feet"* (Acts 4:36–37 NASB).

Nicknames can be very revealing. When people give you a new name, it is usually for a reason. How would you feel if those around you began to call you a son of encouragement?

There are a lot of hurting people around you. If you look hard enough, you might even find one who needs to be encouraged. It might amaze you how much encouragement you might receive in your life by encouraging someone else.

You may have a common name. During this difficult time, why not act in such a way that those around you will think, "He may have a common name, but he (or she) is no common individual"? Become a son of hope, praise, love, or courage. You will never know the impact you will make on the lives of others.

Chapter 56

"These are the times that try men's souls." So wrote Thomas Paine during the dark days of the Revolutionary War. It was those trying times that built our nation's greatest generation. If you are facing a potentially terminal illness, you also are facing trying times. They will be times of pain, tears, stress, grief, and hope. You will find within yourself strength you did not know you had.

The psalmist had a "trying time" experience. He wrote of the people who strengthened him during his struggle, *"As they pass through the Valley of Baca, they make it a place of springs"* (Psalm 84:6a NIV).

One of the characteristics of a desert is a lack of water. This makes travel difficult. It makes walking through a desert nearly impossible. Sometimes generous, gracious individuals would stop in the midst of their travel through the desert and build a well. In the Old Testament, Jacob became famous as a builder of wells. A well is often called an oasis.

Regardless of the valley you are walking through, someone will follow in your steps. That person will experience the same "trying time" you are now experiencing. Why not take this valley experience and build an oasis of hope for the hurting soul who will follow you into this valley? It will make that person's journey a little easier.

Chapter 57

Long-term illness can become a great producer of stress and pressure. Chemotherapy treatments, blood draws, radiation, etc., all become a part of the regular routine. Vacations have to be interrupted or canceled, work plans create conflict as you have to schedule doctor's visits, and bills keep pouring in. More than once I have heard people crack and say, "I can't handle the pressure."

Have you ever had to deal with a flat tire? That is what happens when there is no pressure. Pressure is good. Some stress is motivational. After all, people in comas experience no stress. It is the overload about which you have to be careful. I worked my way through college as an employee of Sears, Roebuck, and Company. They put me in home improvement, divisions 64, 65, and 42. I sold garage door openers, screen doors, garbage disposals, dishwashers, water heaters, and water softeners. The first time I sold a water heater, I learned about a device called a water pressure release valve. It screws into the top of the water heater, and should the pressure inside the tank become too high, it goes off and releases the steam. It keeps the tank from exploding.

You need a pressure release valve. This book was a release valve for me. So is a two- or three-mile walk every morning. For you, it could be a support group associated with the illness you are fighting. It could be a few friends you gather with on a regular basis. It could be kickboxing or karate, making the punching bags your illness. It could be volunteering at a food bank. Whatever works for you, find your release valve.

It would be a shame to survive your illness but suffer a stroke or lose your family. Get help; your family needs you too.

Chapter 58

One of the great transformations in history is that of the Old Testament patriarch Jacob. Jacob was the younger son of Isaac and the grandson of Abraham. His brother Esau was the oldest and was entitled to the bulk of their father's inheritance. However, Jacob, whose name means "schemer," did just that and stole Esau's birthright. Conflict developed, and Jacob fled in fear of Esau's retaliation.

God began to work, and in one of the great stories of the Bible, Jacob wrestled with an angel for an entire evening. Jacob refused to let go until the angel had blessed him. Two things took place.

First, the angel dislocated Jacob's hip. How's that for a blessing? If you are going through the pain of a life-threatening illness, can you think of any blessings that have resulted? It may require some thought, but put your Sherlock Holmes cap on and observe what has transpired over the past few months or years.

Second, God changed Jacob's name to Israel. It was Israel who became the father of the twelve tribes of Israel. Israel means "one who wrestles with God." Have you fought with God over the trial He has brought you to? It is not a sin to do so. To fight, argue, debate, yell, and scream at God are acceptable actions. At the end of all this, we need to yield to His will, but He gives us the right to fight with Him over what is taking place.

If you need to fight with God, He gives you permission. Go ahead and have a knock-down, drag-out fight with Him. Elisabeth Elliot said, "In acceptance there is peace." Let it all out and then accept what happens. It will bring peace to your life.

Chapter 59

Everyone responds to medication in a different way. Nicki's first chemotherapy made her quite ill. After her second treatment, she felt completely drugged. Many who go through this process try to behave in a certain prescribed way. There is no right way to respond. There is only what is. Your body will respond like it responds. There are certain medications that your medical team will give you to overcome whatever negative reactions you had previously, but your body is going to respond in its own way.

I say that to say this. Nicki was having her treatment and met a lady whose mother-in-law climbed Mount Whitney a week after her final treatment. The top of Mount Whitney is the highest point in the continental United States. Most people could not do what she did. Don't try. It is not your task to climb Mount Whitney, to show how tough you are, or to experience no negative reactions. Your only task is to get through this period of time. There will be plenty of time to do what you want to do after everything is finished. Don't be brave, don't be tough, and don't be stoic. Be you. If you get sick, you will get sick. If you feel like crying, cry. You have only one person to whom you must answer, yourself. Your task is to finish.

That is all. In going through chemotherapy, you shouldn't feel any pressure to do anything other than to get through it. If you do that, you have been successful.

Chapter 60

"Warning: This medication can cause mood swings, depression, bloating, and weight gain." Those comforting words were given to us when we purchased Nicki's medication after her fourth chemotherapy treatment. The reason I make mention of the warnings is because Nicki had gained twenty pounds, her face had become bloated, and she had become very depressed. There are two reasons why these warnings are important.

First, if the warnings come true, you won't panic. When Nicki had her biopsy, she had blue dye shot into her blood stream. They told her that for the next several days, her urine would come out blue. When that happened, she didn't panic. Can you imagine the panic if they had not told her and she went to the toilet? Warnings are given for a reason, so that we don't become frightened if the possibility comes to pass.

Second, if the warnings prove true, you can deal with them. Weight gain is a reality when you are on certain medications. Water retention and a host of other issues are just going to happen. In addition, exercise tends to slow down because you are tired. Depression can be overcome through various means. Let me state for the record that some depression is serious and requires medical attention. Your medical team can make recommendations. Much of the depression we see in our culture is temporary and based on negative events in your life. Some of these negative events can be overcome with lots of love and attention, a simple attitude adjustment, and God's special grace. Such was our "depression day."

Nicki was not responding well, and something needed to be done. We decided to go for a walk and stop off for a cup of coffee. As we walked out of the coffee shop, Nicki struck up a conversation with some ladies who were going to be involved in the local "Relay for Life." Their words and actions encouraged her. As we arrived home, we looked in the mailbox and found a big package from Aunt Mary. In it was a quilt made by a co-worker of Mary's who sews them and gives them to cancer survivors. It was beautiful. Another envelope had a $100 check enclosed for Nicki's medical fund. About an hour later, the little girls who live next door to us knocked on the door and handed Nicki a little box. In the box was a bracelet that had a ceramic pink ribbon attached to it. A lady in our church then called up and asked if she could bring in a meal. Our family is quite able to cook for ourselves, but this lady really is a great cook. We forced ourselves to let her come over. The couple who lead the singing for our church each Sunday then stopped by. They had been out of town over the weekend and had picked up a gift basket filled with cheese, smoked salmon, crackers, and sweets.

By the end of the day, Nicki was overwhelmed with people's love and generosity. She still did not feel well, but she had worked through her depression and knew that it would pass. That is a key to recovery. Admit you feel like you do, but understand you will get through the valley.

You may have some people in your sphere of influence who are going through a difficult time. There is something you can do. Fix a meal, bring a fruit basket, give them a call, send them ten dollars, or make them a creative gift. The important thing is not what you do but that you communicate that you care. The other side is also important. If you are hurting, let people minister to you. It will bless you both.

Chapter 61

Elizabeth O'Donnell is a cancer survivor. In 1994, she had a mammogram that showed nothing. A month later, she felt a lump, had a biopsy, was diagnosed with advanced breast cancer, and was given a 5 percent chance of surviving the year. After chemotherapy and a mastectomy, she has been cancer-free for nearly ten years. That is the good news.

Her surviving cancer came at a high price. Six weeks after her final chemo treatment, she had heart failure, which required heart transplant surgery, in 1996. Her heart medication weakened her bones, causing shingles, double pneumonia, kidney disease, and two blood clots.

As they went from one trial to the next, Jim her husband and Elizabeth learned a difficult but important lesson; they communicated differently. Elizabeth wanted to present a happy face, telling people everything was all right. Jim wanted to know and understand everything that was going on. This led to conflict and marriage stress.

Cancer can be a very stressful experience. In one small study, the divorce rate for cancer survivors was much higher than the national average. There are many reasons for this. It is not uncommon for either the cancer survivor or the survivor's mate to go into denial and not want to talk. Finances become stretched. The other person doesn't respond in the "right" way, and hurtful words are exchanged.

Last year, Nicki and I attended an "I Still Do" seminar sponsored by Family Life Today from Little Rock, Arkansas. It is a day-long time of singing and challenging speakers. At the end of the day, each couple is encouraged to take each other's hands and recommit themselves "until death do us part."

That is not difficult at the wedding. It is much more difficult in the midst of a serious illness accompanied by depression, weight gain, hair loss, health problems, and a dozen other difficulties. This is where character matters.

Robert McQuilkin had the right idea. He was the president of Columbia Bible College in South Carolina. He resigned in 1990 because his wife was in the advanced stages of Alzheimer's. He wrote to his friends and stated,

> My dear wife Muriel has been in failing mental health for about eight years. So far, I have been able to carry both her ever-growing needs and my leadership responsibilities at CBC. But recently it has become apparent that Muriel is contented most of the time she is with me and almost none of the time I am away from her. It is not just discontent. She is filled with fear—even terror—that she has lost me and always goes in search of me when I leave home. Then she may be full of anger when she cannot get to me. So it is clear to me that she needs me now, full-time.
>
> Perhaps it would help you to understand if I shared with you what I shared at the time of the announcement of my resignation in chapel. The decision was made, in a way, forty-two years ago when I promised to care for Muriel "in sickness and in health...till death do us part." So, as I told the students and faculty, as a man of my word, integrity has something to do with it. But so does fairness. She has cared for me fully and sacrificially all these years; if I cared for her for the next forty years, I would not be out of her debt. Duty, however, can be grim and stoic. But there is more. I love Muriel. She is a delight to me—her childlike dependence and confidence in me, her warm love, occasional flashes of what I used to relish so, her happy spirit and tough resilience in the face of her continual distressing frustration. I do not have to care for her—I get to! It is a high honor to care for so wonderful a person.

If you are facing the trial of cancer, a good place to begin is to recommit yourselves to each other. Discuss the issues of communication, honor, and fighting fair. It will not make the problems go away, but it will help you to deal with them.

O'Donnell article Wall Street Journal, *September 8, 2004. McQuilkin taken from R. Kent Hughes on biblical disciplines, also quoted by Dennis Rainey.*

Chapter 62

In the last chapter, I mentioned the struggles Jim and Elizabeth McDonnell went through because of the side effects of her cancer. As I read their story in the *Wall Street Journal*, they shared a concept that developed another thought in my mind. I thought you might be helped by running them through your experiences.

The O'Donnells developed what they termed "cancer-free times." When you develop a life-threatening disease, the most common question you hear is, "How are you feeling?" Those closest to you don't need to ask that question, because they see how you are. However, they do want to know what is happening and what they can do to help. It can be a bit overwhelming, so the O'Donnells created their "cancer-free time." It can be anywhere from an hour to a day. You can talk about anything except cancer. In essence, you are asking for a period of time to rest from the obvious. It is not a bad idea, but it must be agreed to and observed by all concerned.

As I read the O'Donnells' story, I noticed a missing piece to the puzzle. It was clear that Jim needed to have more information on what Elizabeth was going through and Elizabeth wanted to be strong and hold it in. They communicated in different ways, and this created tension. In most situations, it is the wife who wants more information and the husband who holds it in.

In addition to the cancer-free time, it would have been beneficial for Jim and Elizabeth to also have a "cancer talk time." It could take place during a walk or drive, having coffee on the patio, or sitting in their favorite chairs in the living room.

Rules would need to be established so that ridicule and badgering don't take place, because the purpose of this time is simply to communicate. Establish a specific amount of time, and then either person can ask any question and the other person needs to answer truthfully and openly. There can be no secrets, and there can be no hard feelings. One person might need to know what is taking place as far as the other's physical health. The other might want to know if there are feelings of leaving or anger taking place. Cancer brings out the best, as in Dr. McQuilkin, and the worst, as in betrayal and abandonment.

The enemy of survival is fear, and that which overcomes fear is knowledge and love. Let your partner know what is taking place, how you feel, and what you expect. You may be expecting something your partner is unable to provide. That is not wrong; it may just be the way it is. It may be that your expectations are unrealistic and need to be adjusted. It may be that your partner is devoted to you but is not as strong as you would like. It may be that you want more information than your partner can give. Talk these issues out. Come to grips, not with what you want, but what is. Remember the words of Elisabeth Elliot: "In acceptance there is peace."

Seek peace and intimacy, not just answers.

Chapter 63

The American Cancer Society has a program that it calls "Look Good... Feel Better." Women going through chemotherapy are invited to a three-hour class in which they are given a professional makeover and $250 worth of make-up and accessories. My wife was invited to one of these classes.

Depression is normal when going through chemotherapy. When Nicki walked into the classroom, she suddenly realized she was going to be among depressed people. Then she understood that this was one of the primary purposes for the class. When chemotherapy is a part of your routine, losing your hair, a bloated face, and weight gain tend to lead to not bothering to use make-up. This then leads to a poor self-image and a decline in romance with your mate.

When Nicki lost her hair, she decided to wear scarves and hats and not a wig. As the class progressed, Nicki decided to take off her scarf and go bald. This began a discussion among the ladies as to their appearances. They all then took off their wigs. As their make-up was being applied, a discussion began over the response of their husbands to their cancer. In almost every case, their husbands were silent, not knowing what to say. This created feelings of being alone on the part of the cancer patients. As the class was finishing up, Nicki looked at one of the ladies and said, "You look very pretty." For the first time that day, she smiled. The "Look Good...Feel Better" class had accomplished its goal.

Is there anything to be learned from this event? Ladies, tell your husbands what you need. Don't leave them to guess as to how to help you. Tell them you need notes of encouragement, kind words, and acts of affection. Buy some new earrings, look for cute outfits; put on some make-up. Even if you don't feel good, you can look as nice as possible. Don't give up.

Chapter 64

The saying "Beauty is in the eyes of the beholder" is really true, especially when it comes to the issue of breast cancer. Men and women are different, and there is no area in which this is more evident than in the area of looks. If a man goes to his high school reunion and someone says "You've gained some weight and lost your hair," it is a joke. Tell a woman she looks fat and the world ends.

When a woman is diagnosed with breast cancer, it is not just a physical problem. It becomes an emotional problem. Some of it is in the DNA. Women need to be told they look pretty. To lose a breast is equated with "I am no longer attractive." Some of it is in our culture, which places such a high value on the perfect body. I shared in an earlier chapter that almost 25 percent of high school senior girls are now being given breast augmentation as graduation gifts. That is not only physically dangerous, but also emotionally destructive. It reemphasizes the stereotype that woman are only attractive if they have a larger bust size.

As we came to the end of Nicki's chemotherapy treatment, she told me she couldn't bring herself to touch her breasts while she took a shower. When I asked her why, she said she was afraid. Obviously, cancer is not physically contagious. It is contagious emotionally. If a woman believes she is no longer attractive, a fork in the road has been reached. Which road she goes down will largely be determined by her husband (or loved ones).

I mentioned in an earlier chapter that your self-image is primarily a result of what you believe those closest to you think of you. There is nowhere this is truer than in this situation. When a woman has been diagnosed with breast cancer, she feels less than sexy. If her husband is turned off by her appearance, that attitude will be confirmed. On the other hand, if the husband steps up and communicates that she is still his # 1 beauty, she will overcome her repulsion of herself.

When I saw what was taking place in Nicki's situation, I got into the shower with her and held her breasts in my hand. I then took her hand and placed it on her breast. She fought me, and then she cried. I continued the process for several days, and she overcame her attitude.

There is no greater fear in the heart of a woman, even the fear of cancer, than the fear of being rejected by her man. This is especially true during cancer treatment. Men, get a grip, yield to God's grace, and make your woman feel like the sexiest woman on earth.

You will never regret it.

Chapter 65

It is called "survivor's guilt" by psychologists. It is what happens when there is an accident and some are hurt or killed and others live. Those who survive often feel guilty for making it while others have lost their lives. It is one of those issues where you know you shouldn't feel this way, but you do.

Nicki was having some problems with her leg, so she scheduled an MRI to see if there was anything that could be done. As she sat in the radiology office, there was another lady with whom Nicki began a conversation. She had gone through several different forms of cancer, each in a different part of the body, and had gone through more than fifty chemotherapy treatments.

As Nicki came home and discussed her day, she began to cry knowing she did not have all of the complications that this woman had experienced. Why God allows some to go through life with few tragedies while others experience multiple disasters is one of the mysteries of life. It is at this point that you need to remember cardinal rule # 3: "Don't ask why; ask, 'What now?'" The truth is, you will never know why one gets cancer, another has a miscarriage, another loses a mate in a car accident, and another seems to have a life minus great tragedies. You will never know, and even if you did, it would not help you cope with life today.

All you can do is live your life in gratitude for the health you do have, the family you still have, and the love of God, which allows you to move forward. You can never know why God has given you another day of life, but you can live it in a way that honors Him and gives meaning to those who have passed on before you.

Chapter 66

We have several new families in our church who have been a blessing to us in our trek toward wellness. Several months ago, one of the ladies called and asked if she could come over and spend some time with Nicki. When she arrived, she was accompanied by a giant picnic basket. Out came the homemade blueberry buckle coffee cake, out came the teapot, and out went the depression.

Cancer can lead to serious bouts with discouragement. There are several actions that can be taken to overcome that depression. Friendship is at the top of the list. A tea party is a great way to demonstrate friendship. If you have a friend who is going through cancer treatment, get out the teapot and make an appointment with your friend. The Bible states that *"a merry heart does good like medicine."*(Proverbs 17:22 NKJV) Tea parties won't cure those battling cancer. However, they will bring healing to the heart, and that is a major part of the healing process.

Order your tea bags now!

Chapter 67

Five days a week, I get up, put on my jogging suit, and walk two or three miles. It is kind of my alone time. I often listen to talk radio programs I have recorded or other pastor's messages I want to glean for a possible sermon. Upon returning home, I usually perk a pot of coffee, jump back in bed, and spend some time talking with Nicki. We close with a time of prayer and get on about the business of the day. Before Nicki was diagnosed, she would sometimes walk with me. About halfway through her chemotherapy, she began to complain about feeling atrophied. Her oncologist recommended she do some stretching exercises, but she needed help.

On my part, I would have to give myself a grade of D minus in helping her exercise. I have no excuse except laziness and forgetfulness. Exercise is a critical part of the healing process. Exercise creates all sorts of positive influences in the body. It also keeps the body limber. Stretching is important to Nicki because she does not have the energy to walk very far.

It would be easy for me to just blame Nicki because she should remind me to help her. However, she is the one who is sick. It is my place to lead in this area. We all fail in one area or another. I failed her in this area. I need to do better. If your loved one is battling with cancer, write a note, set your watch, or call a friend for a wake-up call. Whatever it takes, push your loved one to exercise.

Chapter 68

This past week was probably our worst week since Nicki was diagnosed. It wasn't that anyone tried to do wrong; it's just that everything went wrong. It was the "perfect storm" scenario. When our daughters moved back into the house, we gave each of them certain responsibilities over which they were to keep control. One is to do the grocery shopping and vacuum. The other is responsible for all of the laundry. Later this week, one daughter leaves to fly back to Chicago to be in a wedding. She needed to shop for necessary supplies. The other daughter is involved in a political campaign. She was a political studies major in college and loves the thrill of the battle.

All of the extracurricular activities meant that some things fell through the cracks. Into that mix, add the fact that Nicki had her chemotherapy treatment. When it came time to return to the oncologist, she couldn't find her clothes, the house was messy, and food was sparse in the cupboards.

She suddenly felt overwhelmed by the feeling that she was all alone. The tears flowed, and she wanted to know why she had been abandoned. I don't know what the answer is to this situation. I imagine that sooner or later, everyone who deals with a possibly life-threatening illness will face this situation. Do you quit your job to care for your sick loved one? Do you simply tell him or her, "Chill out, you are overreacting"? Do you have a family meeting and talk through the issue? At this point, I don't have the solution, just the problem. Knowing that this point will come, why not sit down as a family to discuss the adjustments that will need to be made?

It is not a solution for one family member to say, "I don't do sick people very well." Whether you like it or not, it has come your way. Grow up and learn. Another might rationalize and say, "I'm just too busy." It is time to reevaluate your priorities. The one who is sick may wonder why everyone else isn't at his or her every beck and call. Lighten up. The world will not end if there are dishes in the sink.

Set up regular family meetings and talk about the issues of life and death. Just a reminder, everyone wants it to be like it was.

It isn't, so accept that and "do the next thing."

Chapter 69

My mother was recently diagnosed with breast cancer. She has chosen a different path from ours. She is seventy-seven years old, has a husband who is in the early stages of Alzheimer's, and does not have the support system we have. She has agreed to surgery and to radiation, but she has rejected any chemotherapy. We might do it differently than she would, but she is making those decisions for herself, and we will abide by her decision.

When I talked with her as she faced her surgery, two things came to the surface. First, her attitude is "Whatever the doctor says is all right with me." I understand that attitude. I now know where I developed that same mindset. Second, I am grateful we made the decisions we made.

I mentioned in a previous chapter the importance of second opinions. In discussing my mother's situation with her, I realized a reason why we got a second opinion. After Dr. Chong came into the waiting room to give us the results of Nicki's surgery, he made a statement that did not register at that time. He mentioned that he removed the tumor, sent it to pathology, and waited for their report. They called and said that the margins on the tumor were not wide enough and he should remove a little more tissue. He went back in and did as he was advised.

When we went in for our second opinion, Dr. Chawla examined Nicki's surgical records and mentioned how impressed he was that the surgeon had waited for the pathologist's report before ending surgery. It seems that the popular procedure now is to remove the tumor, send it to pathology, stitch up the patient, send the patient home, get the pathology report, and schedule a second surgery if the margins aren't right. There may be many reasons why the doctor decides to go with this plan. Be sure to ask about the reasons for what he or she does.

I mention this because my mother called to inform me that they are scheduling her for a second surgery. Had we not gotten a second opinion, we would not have known about this practice. If you are facing cancer surgery, it is your right to ask which practice your surgeon goes by. Just a reminder, you need to make this decision, not your doctor. If he plans on scheduling you for a second surgery instead of waiting, you might want to check out another surgeon. You are not paying him to work you into his convenient schedule. You are hiring him to heal you and to give you peace of mind. You have the right to make this decision.

Thank you, Dr. Chong, for putting us first.

Chapter 70

Do you know people who rub you the wrong way? Deborah is a critical part of our recovery team, and she rubs Nicki the right way. Deborah is a masseuse, and she works out Nicki's kinks, knots, and stresses. Nicki has had a bad back for a long time, but since she was diagnosed with cancer, her knees and legs have caused her some problems. Deborah helps to work out those aches and pains.

Everyone is different. I do not like backrubs. I do not get tense. I tend to be relaxed most of the time. If someone gives me a backrub, it is painful. Nicki is not like me. She does get tense, and her body does need a massage. Remember that cardinal rule #10 states "Get through the bad days." Your goal, as I stated in the last chapter, is to get through this period of time. If you gain weight, so be it. If you spend a little too much money, get back on track tomorrow. If you feel the need to have a second opinion, get it. If you need a night out, take it. If you need a massage, make the call. It is not an unnecessary expenditure if it puts you in a good mood. It is a temporary necessity.

Chapter 71

I was asked the other day if I was angry about Nicki's cancer. I don't know what it says about me, but I am not. It may be my passive personality, or it may be that I understand the destructive nature of anger. There is a place for anger. We should be angry at injustice and evil. Illnesses, on the other hand are a part of life. If you need to get angry at your illness, go ahead. However, find a way to deal with it in a positive way. Go to the gym and punch a bag, step into the backyard and scream, or go for a walk. Don't do what is normally done; don't take your anger out on those around you.

If I feel anything, it is tired. I wake up several times a night to go to the restroom. I almost always go right back to sleep. If I stay awake more than fifteen minutes, I put on my jogging suit and walk two miles. It is my way of dealing with my frustrations. It also makes me easier to live with. During Nicki's last chemotherapy session, I saw a plaque on the wall.

> Cancer is so limited.
> It cannot shatter hope.
> It cannot corrode faith.
> It cannot destroy faith.
> It cannot kill friendship.
> It cannot suppress memories.
> It cannot silence courage.

>It cannot invade the soul.
>It cannot steal eternal life.
>It cannot conquer the soul.
>—Anonymous

There is a place for anger. There is also a place for acceptance and gratitude for what an illness cannot do. That leads to peace, and I choose to live there.

Chapter 72

There are three aspects to cancer therapy: surgery, chemotherapy, and radiation. Chemotherapy seeks to kill every cancer cell in the body. In our case, it involved six separate treatments, was taken through an IV, and usually occurred every three weeks. Chemotherapy is taken every three weeks and lasts about three hours per treatment. Radiation usually takes place over a seven-week span, is administered five days per week, and takes about fifteen minutes per treatment. (This of course is prescribed individually on a case by case basis.)

Radiation treatment is much different. Rather than medicine injected into the body, radiation is an x-ray beam that is aimed at specific parts of the body. While chemotherapy is aimed at the body in general, radiation is isolated to the specific area around where the tumor was removed.

The process in Nicki's treatment was very high tech. It almost appears like something out of a science fiction movie. Everything is programmed by a computer, and technicians administer the x-ray beam radiation therapy treatment.

The effects of chemotherapy and radiation are totally different procedures, both physically and emotionally. Chemotherapy, in layman's terms, is poisoning your body to kill any remaining cancer cells. It can make you physically ill. Nicki was able to get out and do some things during the third week after each treatment, but the first two weeks were times to rest when needed. Radiation has a much different effect. Radiation can drain you physically but is much more problematic emotionally.

Radiation has two primary side effects: it makes you tired, and it can burn the skin. We were able to deal with Nicki's being tired by scheduling her treatments at 2:30 p.m. It allowed Nicki to work in the morning, have her treatment in the afternoon, and rest in the evening.

Nicki's first day of radiation did not go well, it was quite traumatic. What was supposed to be a thirty to forty-five minute appointment turned into two hours. Nicki's technicians, Raja and Adrianna, were both professional and compassionate. They showed her the table on which she would lie down and explained the procedure. The computer is used to line up the precise angle of the beam. The only way to effectively set the angle is to mark up the breast, analyze the tumor area, and plot the process of shooting the area to destroy any cancer cells that might have survived chemotherapy. Marks would be drawn on her breast to give the technicians a visualization of where to aim the x-ray beam. The doctor would come in to check the angles, not being satisfied with the way it lined up the technicians would have to start the process all over again. In the conversation, one of the technicians mentioned to Nicki that they would "tattoo" her breast to make their identification of the location easier. That made her very nervous. We are not big fans of tattoos and didn't like that idea. Do you remember our ten cardinal rules? The first one says, "Stay in control." Rather than get frustrated and annoyed at the technicians, we chose to deal with this in a positive manner by looking for a creative alternative. We simply asked Raja and Adrianna to refer to the marks as "markers," not "tattoos." No offense was taken on their part, and none was given on ours. It was a win-win proposition. By the time she was finished, she looked like one of those diagrams you see at the butcher shop that outline where different selections of meat come from. This procedure is necessary, but it can be very degrading.

The question every patient asks is probably "Why can't they do it differently?" The answer simply is, they can't. In order to be precise, the technicians have to have marks by which they can determine angles and depths. This is just something that has to be done. There is no way around it.

Dr. Victor Schweitzer was our radiation oncologist. He is a brilliant doctor, but just as important, he is patient-friendly. He was the doctor who fit us into his schedule right after Nicki was diagnosed, even though he was leaving the next day for vacation. We met with Dr. Schweitzer each Monday after Nicki's treatment and were given as much time as necessary to discuss any issue that we had.

There is an old adage that can help. The saying "To be forewarned is to be forearmed" is really true. A woman cannot prevent the humiliation of having her breast marked up, but being forewarned, she can at least be prepared. Plan an overnighter at a nice bed and breakfast location. Go out on a romantic date. Walk on the beach. See a play. Whatever you really enjoy doing, plan for that evening. Just a reminder, there are many aspects of recovery that are painful, humiliating, and unpleasant. Your goal is not to enjoy them, but to get through them. Your radiation treatments will be unpleasant, but you will get through them.

That should be an encouraging thought!

Chapter 73

I mentioned that one of the negative consequences of radiation is the burn marks left by the treatments. During our first meeting with Dr. Schweitzer after our treatments had begun, we mentioned how pleased we were that Nicki's skin had not experienced any burn marks. He prepared us by saying it would not remain like that, and he was right.

The skin around the breast will become red and very tender. In Nicki's case, the skin around her armpit became very brown. Every situation will be a little different because every tumor is a different size and in a different location. However, after thirty-five treatments, the skin will begin to burn sometime and in some location.

When the burning began, Dr. Schweitzer recommended that we go to the drugstore and purchase some aloe vera gel. There are two different types of aloe vera gel. One has alcohol in it, and the other is 99 percent pure aloe vera. Don't get the one with alcohol, because it irritates the skin. After about fifteen treatments, Nicki's skin was really burned, and Dr. Schweitzer ordered some hydrocortisone cream. Here is a recommendation. Begin from day one to anoint the area with plenty of aloe vera gel. It will probably not prevent the burning, but it will delay the pain and quicken the healing process.

Chapter 74

When it rains, it pours. That old adage certainly seems to prove correct. Halfway through Nicki's radiation treatment, her teeth began to bother her, and a root canal was necessary. When she arrived home, her entire arm was black and blue. This concerned us, so we made an appointment with our oncologist, who is also a hematologist. They took blood, had it analyzed, and informed us that Nicki's red platelet count was low. Blood platelets are the cells that allow for blood clotting and also prevent bruising. A normal count is 135,000-400,000. Nicki registered 25,000 platelets. They asked us to return the next day to discern which way the count was going, and she registered 22,000 platelets.

We were told by some people that this is not uncommon. Our oncologist disagreed. The white cells see the platelets as a foreign presence and begin their seek-and-destroy mission.

Nicki was admitted to the hospital, had a transfusion of red blood platelets, and tested at 40,000 two days later. It was still low, but the downward slide had ceased and the number was increasing.

Just a trivia fact: red blood platelets are yellow.

Chapter 75

I write the songs that make the whole world sing.
I write the songs of love and special things.
I write the songs that make the young girls cry.
I write the songs, I write the songs.

My home lies deep within you, and I've got my home in your heart.
Now when I look out through your eyes,
I am young again even though I am old.
…I am music and I write the song.

So wrote Barry Manilow in his famous "I Write the Songs." Music has had a powerful impact on people for thousands of years. The Old Testament tells the story of King Saul, who was being emotionally and spiritually oppressed. Saul called for a young shepherd boy named David to come and sing songs to him. David's music brought comfort and calmness to the depressed king.

Throughout history, music has shown a tremendous power to move a culture. Whether it was the pounding drums in Africa, the protest songs of the 1960's, or the patriotic songs during the Revolutionary, Civil, and two world wars, music moves people. The song "Happy Days are Here Again" was specifically written to get people's hopes up during the depths of the Depression. The longest book in the Bible is primarily a songbook called "Psalms."

When going through a serious illness, it is very easy to sing the old spiritual "Nobody Knows the Trouble I've Seen." While there is a place for that music, there is so much more. Some classical music can truly calm the soul. Instrumental mood music can bring comfort and peace. For the believer, there are many resources available to buy music filled with praise and worship songs. What a wonderful time you could have as you are flat on your back to simply listen to music that elevates the soul and the spirit, and that brings peace to the heart. Many of the great hymns have been penned by people going through the most difficult of times. "It Is Well with My Soul" was a hymn written by a man contemplating the loss of his wife and children after their ship went down at sea.

Why not write the songs of your heart? Whether anyone else ever reads or sings them is unimportant. They would be songs about times of great discouragement and times of incredible joy. They would open up your heart to experiencing God in a whole new way. Many of them would bless and encourage your friends and family.

Where to start? Why not read through the book of Psalms and get a feel for the emotions that are expressed in those 150 songs? Then write what is in your heart. It will be a remarkable journey for you and those around you.

Chapter 76

One of the side effects of going through trials is the opportunity given to others to do well on your behalf. In many cases, people will come up with some very creative ways to minister to your needs or to help someone else in your name.

Several years ago, we became foster parents. It only lasted one year, but we still treat Kathryn as our daughter, and she introduces us as her mom and dad. During the Christmas season, Nicki and I were invited to her home for an open house. With her gift was a card that read,

> I will be donating blood platelets in your honor
> on January 3 from 9:00 a.m. to 11:00 a.m.
> Merry Christmas!
>
> Love,
> Kathryn

I am a regular blood donor to the American Red Cross. It never would have occurred to me to encourage someone to give platelets. However, because the life expectancy for platelets is less than a week, they are always in short supply. You could call today to make an appointment. It truly is giving the gift of life. It just might give someone many more Christmases and birthdays.

Chapter 77

It was a day of tears. Nicki went into the radiation room, lay down on the table, and started to cry. Treatment number thirty-six. Last day. She left the doctor's office and headed for her physical therapy. She got onto the table and began to cry. When she arrived home and began to talk about her day, she began to cry. It had been a long ordeal and was finally coming to an end.

At seven p.m., ten or fifteen dear friends knocked on the door. I had ordered a cake and dropped it off at a friend's house to bring with them when they came, and it was celebration time. Nicki doesn't like surprises, but this worked out well. It was just a time to celebrate life. The Jews have a phrase, *l'chaim*. It simply means "to life." The Bible tells us to "weep with those who weep and rejoice with those who rejoice." This was a night to do both.

L'chaim!

Chapter 78

Bills, bills, and more bills. I have never been seriously ill. When our children were born, we had two primary debts: the hospital and the doctor. With Nicki's cancer treatments, we had bills coming from everywhere. We have insurance, and they treated us very well. We also have a large deductible. This meant that many of the doctor's visits came out of our pocket. There was also the benefit of money being raised for our medical expenses by friends and family. I love to study, but bookkeeping is not my strength.

Our friend Kathleen is a CPA and also the treasurer for our church. She does a great job of keeping our church books and also handled all of the contributions that came in on our behalf. After Nicki's surgery, Kathleen came to us and asked if we would like her to handle all of the financial aspects of Nicki's care. A few days later, she came over and showed us a spreadsheet for our income and billing. When a bill arrives, we simply hand it to her, and she records the information. If there is money in the account, she pays the bill. If necessary, she deducts it from my salary. In either case, I do not have to worry about whether the billing is accurate or current. I read an article several years ago that stated that the average medical bill has a 5 to 10 percent discrepancy. Because of Kathleen's expertise, we are free of any billing problems.

There are many ways to help someone going through a serious illness. Raising money is obviously helpful. Meals, cards, notes, and visits are also a blessing. If you have bookkeeping and accounting skills, make yourself available. You will probably take a big load off of the person's and the family's back as well.

Chapter 79

Several years ago, Nicki and I became concerned about our weight and did something about it. Joining one of the largest weight loss groups in our nation, we both lost more than thirty pounds over the next year. After Nicki was diagnosed with cancer, we dropped out of the meetings. There were many reasons we stopped attending meetings. None of them could stand up to true criticism, but cancer causes one to change one's priorities.

Nicki went back to her meeting this past week. She is back on track and losing weight. Her leader asked her to take a moment and share her story. There were few dry eyes at her meeting. At the end of the meeting, a woman came up to her, thanked her for her words, and said, "I'm a nine-year survivor."

Words have an incredible power to encourage or destroy. Take the opportunities you are given to speak healing to others. Solomon wrote, *"death and life are in the power of the tongue, and those who love it will eat its fruit."* (Proverbs 18:21 NASB) You will never look back on your life and regret saying words of encouragement to those going through difficult times. Learn to enjoy the fruit of a kind word.

Chapter 80

Bald is beautiful. At least, that is what those who have lost their hair say. God invented hair for those who don't have perfect heads. Yul Brynner, Telly Savalas, Ving Rhames, and Vin Diesel are just a few of the actors who have made a career of playing bald, tough guys.

For some reason, women losing their hair doesn't have the sexy image that it has for men. Nicki, of course, is the exception. She looked really sexy. She also really loved the freedom of not being a slave to her hair. She could walk out of the shower and dry her head, and she was ready to go.

After chemotherapy, her hair began to grow back. Decisions, decisions, decisions. Every cancer survivor is different. Some women find their hair grows back exactly as it was before. Some find their hair grows back gray or white. Some find their straight hair grows back curly.

I have a picture of Nicki on my desk that was taken nearly thirty years ago. She was in a group of two hundred college students who rode their bikes from Monterey to Disneyland. Her hair is long, layered, and very pretty.

Having gone bald, she really loved the convenience of not having to spend time on her hair. As she began to decide what to do, a funny pattern developed. Many would say, "I love your hair. Leave it just like it is." Others said, "Gray hair makes you look older." Others said, "Tinting your hair gets very expensive." After surveying dozens of friends and family, we came to the conclusion that there was no consensus. The fact is, everyone has an opinion and is willing to share it.

Bottom line: do what you like. Do you like it long, short, weaved, tinted, or permed? Do what you want. Go back to cardinal rule #9: "Be gracious to the stupid people in your world." The only one who has to deal with your decision is you. It is not a spiritual or a moral issue—it is a preference. Ask for people's comments, check with the professionals, and then do what you like. Don't let others control your life.

P.S. Just a reminder. After you have your hair done, if you don't like it, change it!

Chapter 81

We decided to spend the first year anniversary of Nicki's mammogram in Hawaii. Some friends recommended a hotel, and the arrangements were made. As we prepared ourselves for the trip, there were two concerns. First was Nicki's platelet count. Second was her next mammogram. We had both tests scheduled just before we were to leave. Her platelet count registered 126,000. With the goal being 140,000 and her count increasing about 5,000 each week, the doctor gave us the green light. Nicki then received a letter from the Nancy Reagan Breast Center. It read in part, "The above breast examination did not show any sign of cancer, according to the radiologist's interpretation."

Life will probably never be "normal" again, but we can get on with our lives and be grateful for health.

L'chaim!

Chapter 82

What if it comes back? That question lies in the heart of every cancer survivor. It may cause more fear than the original question of "What if I get cancer?" After all of her treatments, Nicki had mammograms on a regular basis. Almost a year after her last treatment, she had a mammogram that showed a spot. A biopsy was needed, but it took almost two weeks to get an appointment. It was a physically painful experience for Nicki and took three days before the tests came back. Nicki referred to it as "Black Wednesday." Dr. Schweitzer called Thursday morning and simply said, "It's good news!" He didn't need to say more.

In our travel through this valley, we met people who went through reoccurrences. It was obviously a very depressing situation. What would we have done? The same thing we did at the beginning of this journey. We would *do the next thing*.

Chapter 83

Remember our discussion about our oncology nurse who said that the port-a-cath was "no big deal"? Shortly after everything was complete and no further tests were needed, Nicki came down with a severe case of bronchitis. Fearing it might go into pneumonia, our doctor scheduled a chest x-ray.

The radiologist walked into our room and said, "It is bronchitis. Did you know that you have a plastic tube lodged in your chest?" We didn't know what he was talking about, so we began a discussion with him. Nicki said "No but I did have a port-a-cath removed." The doctor showed us the x-ray and there it was. A portion of the port-a-cath tube had broken off when it was removed and was still in the vein.

Our oncology medical team assured us this presented no danger. To us this was a big deal, so an additional surgery had to be scheduled to remove the remnant of tubing. Just take this as a reminder that any medical procedure has risks, and could have serious complications. You don't need to become anxious or paranoid, but you do need to treat everything as a big deal. It is your body. It is your life.

Chapter 84

Death.

This is the chapter Nicki asked me not to write. However, it needs to be said. Death is the subject most people don't want to talk about. I am not quite sure why that is; it is so much a part of our lives. We take out life insurance policies, immunize our children from diseases, and attend funerals. The Bible simply states, "It is appointed unto man once to die." When I officiate at funerals, I always make the point that while life expectancy has increased, the death rate is still one per person. Every one of us will one day be the focal point of a funeral service.

Cancer is only one way people die. Some die from their battle with cancer. Many survive cancer and die from another illness. We have friends who went through leukemia with their four-year-old daughter. She survived and will probably live to be eighty-five. One day, she too will die.

We battle cancer because life is worth living. While we understand that death will come, today we choose life! That is why God sent His Son into this world, to release us from the fear of death. Christmas, Good Friday, and Easter are all a part of God's plan to deal with the consequences of death. Death is a reality, but it is not the rest of the story. When Jesus emerged from the tomb on Easter Sunday, He put death to death and brought forth life.

As we began our journey through the "valley of the shadow of death," we realized that death was a possibility. We resisted that with every fiber of our being. Not because we feared death, but because we love life. Moses stated thousands of years ago, "I have set before you life and death; choose life." We have bought into his wisdom. The thought of leaving behind our loved ones was too painful to imagine. However, we had made peace with God many years ago. We committed our lives to Him, followed His will for our lives, and loved Him with all of our hearts.

We have survived cancer. We have many more days before us, for which we are grateful. But the goal of life is not merely to die old. The psalmist wrote, *"Teach us to number our days that we may present to You a heart of wisdom"* (Psalms 90:12 NASB). We have sought to live wisely.

C. S. Lewis is one of the most beloved writers of the twentieth century. His books *The Lion, the Witch, and the Wardrobe* and *Prince Caspian* have been read by millions and have both been made into full-length movies. The seventh and final tale in the Chronicles of Narnia series is entitled *The Last Battle*. It ends with these words:

> And as he spoke, he no longer looked to them like a lion; but the things that began to happen after that were so great and beautiful that I cannot write them. And for us this is the end of all the stories, and we can most truly say that they all lived happily ever after. But for them, it was only the beginning of the real story. All their life in this world and all their adventures in Narnia had only been the cover and the title page; now at last they were beginning Chapter One of the Great Story which no one on earth has read; which goes on forever; in which every chapter is better than the one before.

Nicki and I anticipate a long life together. We look forward to grandchildren, our fiftieth anniversary, and our hundredth birthdays. However, we know that one day life as we know it will come to an end, and life as He knows it will begin.

We are ready!

Jackson Family Pictured from Left to Right Glen, Ashley, Erin, Nicki

Epilogue

by
Nicki Jackson

Do the Next Thing

On Valentine's Day, I was working in my home office when Glen came in and handed me a Valentine's Day greeting card. There was nothing unusual about him giving me a card because he was always a thoughtful person. Each Valentine's Day, he would do something special like dinner out at a nice restaurant, tickets to a concert, or dinner theater. Sometimes, he invited me for a long walk on the beach. These activities were often accompanied by a bouquet of flowers. He liked to give me an "experience" as opposed to jewelry or some such gift. Glen always took time to nurture our marriage. I opened the card while he watched, looking very pleased with himself. I spotted a check tucked inside the card and thoughts started flooding my mind such as, "He is giving me money. Maybe he wants me to buy clothes!" When I unfolded the check, it was made payable to the Nancy Reagan Breast Center. In the memo line, it was neatly printed, "For a mammogram." I remember looking at him, trying to keep my feelings in check. I inquired as to what the check was for. I was perplexed by this strange gift. There had been no conversation regarding a need for a mammogram. He stated that he couldn't think of what to get me for Valentine's Day and thought a mammogram was something I needed to have done. I was working hard and hadn't made an appointment for my yearly routine x-rays. I had my first mammogram two years prior and hadn't made an appointment since. Glen said he had gone to the Breast Center and asked if they had gift certificates. They looked at him strangely and politely said "no." He asked how much the mammogram cost and made out the check for that amount of money. I really had to act as though I was grateful for the gift, but inside I didn't think it was very romantic or exciting. Life was an adventure with Glen, and I never knew what he would come up with. However, this was the strangest of them all. When I called the Nancy Reagan Breast Center to make an appointment, they asked me, "Do you have any symptoms?" I said no and made my appointment for April.

The day of that mammogram appointment would change my life forever. After taking several x-rays, the technician asked me to step into another room for an ultrasound. There it was—a mass under the nipple on the right breast. My heart sank, and the nightmare began with the unknown. The radiologist could not tell me anything or answer any of my questions. I would need to talk with my doctor to see what I needed to do next. A biopsy was scheduled and the procedure done. I had to wait to hear the results. The diagnosis was in: "You have breast cancer." Following were surgery, chemotherapy, and radiation. My husband saved my life with that unusual gift. (The next year for Valentine's Day, he asked if I wanted a colonoscopy!) He didn't lose his sense of humor even when we didn't feel like laughing. It did make me smile. The cancer was an aggressive form, and we had caught it early!

One day, I realized that all of the attention was on me and I had not asked my husband how he was doing. I asked Glen how he was dealing with all that we were experiencing. His response was, "I am writing a book." He said he had just finished chapter three.

"What are you writing about?" I asked.

"The fear of cancer," he stated. Glen named the book *Do the Next Thing*.

"Do the next thing" is what I have to live each day doing, regardless of the circumstances.

I remember the day I sat in a shopping center parking lot contemplating the fact that my hair was going to fall out. The question in my mind was, should I cut my long hair short in anticipation of what was to come? Maybe it would be less traumatic? The answer was yes. I called my hair stylist, and she told me to come right over to the salon. When I walked in, a man from our church was sitting in the stylist's chair getting a buzz haircut. I saw him and burst out with a loud cry with tears streaming down my cheeks. I scared everyone in the salon, and all eyes were on me. My stylist held me in her arms while I cried and composed myself. The poor client in the chair looked bewildered. That was the beginning of feeling vulnerable. The next week, my hair began to fall out in the shower. My stylist came to the house to buzz the rest of my hair. As each lock of hair fell to the floor, I felt a piece of myself surrendering to what was to be. I had cancer and couldn't change the next steps of the journey.

People always call it a journey, but I think of it as a battle, and you have to win! I had to trust the medical professionals with expertise in ridding my body of cancer. It was explained to me that the cancer cells can travel to other parts of your body and set up camp. This was a visual I kept in my mind's eye as I did battle quickly and decisively to keep the cancer from spreading. Cut it out, burn it out, poison it out, and do whatever it takes. I got weaker and weaker but continued to work when I could. The radiation burned a hole in my skin, and I was given ointments to sooth the area. I used aloe vera gel to spread over the area every day. I did this for a long time, even after the treatments. Did it help? I don't know, but it gave me control over my own body. Spreading the aloe gel gave me a feeling of being proactive in the battle. All I knew was it couldn't hurt to use the gel. Keeping some control in the process became important to me. Sometimes this just came by asking questions to get a better understanding of what was to happen next and why.

All the while, I clung to the Scripture Philippians 4:13 NKJV: *"I can do all things through Christ who strengthens me."* "Do the next thing" is a quote, a mantra I have to live by when the "suddenlys" of life come. I was privileged to travel to Israel several years back with a group of pastors and wives. When we were in Tiberius on the Sea of Galilee, we gathered on the beach one evening to sing praise songs. The sky was clear, the water still, and the moon illuminated the night. It was such a peaceful and beautiful experience. When I awoke in the early morning hours, I heard the wind whipping against the side of the building. A torrential storm was raging on the sea. It came up without any warning. It was raining, waves were raging, and palm trees were bending near the ground. What had happened? One minute, complete peace and contentment; life is good. The next minute, life is raging out of control. This is what I refer to as the "suddenlys" of life." When everything is normal, beautiful, peaceful, and suddenly the news reaches you. The phone rings, the report comes in, and your life is turned upside down. You can't breathe. Fear grips you. Words are spoken—"You have breast cancer"—and unfamiliar terminology is used, and you have lost control. What do you say? What do you do? How do you gain control? Your life as you know it is disrupted! Psalm 61 says, "Let me take refuge under the shelter of your wings." (Psalms 61:4, ESV)

It seemed as though the storm of one treatment and appointment after another was over. I was cancer-free! My body was ravaged, and now it was time for building me back up. I pushed myself to swim, walk, and breathe deeply. My brain was in a fog commonly referred to as "chemo brain," and when my family got frustrated with me for repeating myself, I explained I was trying to cement what I was supposed to remember in my head. I asked them to be kind to me, and they seemed to understand. Each day I got stronger and stronger and felt more "normal."

Life would never be the same, but we got through it together. It made us stronger and more tolerant of each other and helped us to appreciate what was important in life.

One August day, Glen and I left for church to participate in an early morning prayer meeting in our little chapel from 6:00 a.m. to 7:00 a.m. We were joined by my son-in-law Lance and daughter Erin to pray together for one hour. Erin wanted to sleep in that morning, but Lance encouraged her to go. When the prayer time was over, Erin left for work. Lance, Glen, and I decided to go out to breakfast. It was a beautiful, sunny day, and going out seemed the thing to do since we hadn't eaten yet. There was a little café where we liked to have breakfast right around the corner, and I don't remember what Lance or I ordered, but Glen ordered oatmeal and toast. He was always trying to take care of himself. Besides, he was participating in an extreme boot camp military-style exercise class. The guys were joking around, and I thought it was nice they had such a special relationship. Our church employed Lance as our youth minister while he was going to Bible college. It was a relationship not many fathers-in-law have the opportunity to experience. After we finished with our breakfast, the three of us went back to the church, and Lance left us there alone. Glen said he would unlock my office and then went into his office. While I was turning on my computer, Glen walked by my window, and a few minutes later, my cell phone rang. It was Glen saying he was in the children's building and he needed my help. He seemed calm, but there was something in his voice—I knew something was wrong. All I could think of was blood. I grabbed my phone, keys, and purse, thinking I would need to drive him to the hospital. When I reached the children's building and unlocked the door, Glen was leaning against the wall. I asked him, "What's wrong?" He said he was numb all over. I asked him what he thought it was as I was dialing 9-1-1. He said he thought he was having a stroke. I could hear the sirens in the distance.

I stroked his head and told him, "Don't be afraid." The sirens got closer, and I had to leave him to let the paramedics know where he was located. Glen was taken to the hospital, and when he arrived, he went into a coma. When Glen slipped into the coma, Simi Valley had an earthquake at that moment. Glen would have loved that! The emergency room doctor told me Glen needed a neurosurgeon, and he needed to get Glen "the hell out of there fast!" He was airlifted to a trauma center, and I was told a blood vessel had burst at the base of his brain stem and the blood needed to be stopped because it was destroying his brain. While I sat in Glen's room and watched the monitors, I would ask God, "Why?" He would keep giving me the same answer: "Why not you?" I didn't like God's answer, but I understood it. I had been with many people over the years, praying with them and holding them while a loved one slipped away or suffered from a serious sickness or accident. It was my turn! I didn't like it! I hated it! But I understood it. A large group of people gathered each day to watch, wait, and pray for Glen to recover. In the book of Isaiah, it says Jesus was a man of sorrow, acquainted with grief. The savior didn't like going to the cross, but He understood it. He understood my fears and the grief that engulfed me, and that gave me comfort. Eleven days later, while family surrounded Glen's hospital bed and sang praise songs, he went home to be with the Lord.

What were my new marching orders? We were married thirty years and worked in ministry thirty-five years together. My best friend and prayer partner was gone, and my role in the church had changed. What now? Glen wrote this book for all of you struggling with the fear of cancer, and it has become a love story for me. My prayer is that, regardless of what your fears are and your story is, you will put one foot in front of the other each day and "Do the next thing."

Notes

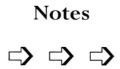

Chapter 58 and Chapter 62:
1. References to Elisabeth Elliot *Loneliness* / Elisabeth Elliot by Elliot, Elisabeth
   ISBN 0-8407-9098-8 hc
2. Quote from the book Loneliness: "In acceptance there is peace" referenced in Elisabeth Elliot book used with permission from Amy Carmichael, *Toward Jerusalem* (copyright 1936 Dohnavur Fellowship; Ft. Washington, PA: Christian Literature Crusade, Inc.; London: S.P.C.K.) "For in Acceptance lieth peace")

Acknowledgements

Melinda Hughes, Graphic Artist
Carolyn Philmon for helping make this book possible
Jennifer Inman for technical skills
Ashley Jackson for persistent encouragement
My daughters Erin, Ashley, and Kathryn for your love and support
My Son-in-law Lance Skifter, he had big shoes to fill

"Thank you" two simple words just don't seem enough.
"I love you from the top of the sky, to the bottom of the ocean. And that's a whole lot of love!"

Nicki

CPSIA information can be obtained
at www.ICGtesting.com
Printed in the USA
FSOW01n2317260815
10354FS